WHAT PE

"Our law enforcement officers are not taken care of the way most people think, particularly when it comes to their mental health. In Invisible Wounds, author and former police officer Nicholas Anthony takes the reader through a different kind of story—an experience not often relayed via the mainstream media, who have continually ignored the critical law enforcement issues of post-traumatic stress disorder and suicide.

Anthony skillfully explains the depths to which a police officer can fall, utilizing his own story, as we learn the potential root causes of PTSD after a long career experiencing ugly and unnerving scenarios courtesy of the public of whom law enforcement officers typically meet on their very worst days. Some believe our law enforcement officers suffer as a result of one defining critical incident, such as an officer-involved shooting. And though this can certainly be the case, the more common cause of PTSD is consistent exposure to more routine, yet equally as impactful, calls such as dead bodies, suicides, domestic violence, sex crimes, and a never-ending supply of reminders as to the horrific actions human beings are capable of. This is called cumulative trauma, and Anthony describes it with the deft touch of someone who not only has experienced these calls, but suffers from them greatly

Beginning with his time in the United States Army's ROTC program, Anthony paints a picture of a man who simply wanted to serve. A true hero in the making whose goals centered around helping the people in his community through selfless service. It's the calling many of us have, but unfortunately the job often does not match our expectations when the realities of police work begin to unceremoniously present themselves.As we learn of his experiences in the police academy, Anthony highlights what law enforcement officers are taught in order to both survive in a tactical sense, as well as in dealing with a demanding public whose views of the police are often jaded by perceptions manufactured by the media. All of this culminates in a first act that meticulously describes his time as a new officer while riding with a field training officer. His time training to be a police officer, while informative, is also a startling look at the indoctrination process into police culture in America.

At its core, *Invisible Wounds* is the heartfelt story of a police officer who arrived into the profession with the intention to do good for people, but was systematically torn down as he found difficulty in coping with the brutal and violent world he had been thrust into with no warning from his trainers or superiors as to how this job can break you. And unlike many texts that have thoughtfully covered this subject, Anthony's book is devoid of a just one singular incident affecting his mental health, instead laying out in detail the dozens of incidents and interactions during a fifteen-year career that took an undeniable toll on his ability to perform the job. All the while, his cries for help were ignored by an agency completely unprepared to take care of their own."

Jason Harney, Producer/Director, *The Wounded Blue*, Producer/Director/Editor/Writer, Lightning Digital Entertainment, Las Vegas Police Sergeant (Retired)

"*Invisible Wounds* invites readers to join the author on his personal journey of faith. Through storytelling, he tears down every emotional wall within and becomes vulnerable. As you turn the pages, he humbly describes his constant battle with conflicts, cynicism, and trauma on the job that led to his burnout and post-traumatic stress diagnosis. His stories are filled with sadness and struggle, but through his faith in God, he found the light that ultimately led him to a place of peace where he now resides. This is a must-read for all first responders, families of first responders, and supporters of first responders."

Tamara Mickelson, author, *Through My Eyes: CSI Memoirs That Haunt the Soul*, Sergeant, Sacramento County Sheriff's Department (Retired)

"*Invisible Wounds* relates one man's experience pursuing God in the midst of a very real battle with the evil he confronts as a police officer in a small rural community. Follow Nick as he takes you through his early experiences in the Army National Guard and career in law enforcement, including his battle with PTSD. Nick relates some of the lighter moments during his twelve-year career, but also paints a graphic—and sometimes disturbing—picture of police work. Some stories he relays will make you laugh, and others will make you cry. This book serves as a sober reminder of the physical, emotional, and spiritual challenges encountered by police and all first responders in this country.

Although Nick's personal journey takes him through some very dark valleys, he provides hope to many of our brave heroes suffering a similar fate as a result of their commitment to serve and protect the most vulnerable among us. PTSD does not strike only combat veterans but is a very real threat to anyone who deals daily with the stressors associated with violence, suffering, and death.

I highly recommend this book to anyone in policing or emergency service careers … or the family members backing those who are. At a time when the very concept of law and order is under great attack, we need—now more than ever—to support our selfless men and women on the front lines."

Amy Travis, author, *You Can Visit, but You Can't Live There: Keys to Living Free from Fear, Anxiety, and Guilt*

INVISIBLE WOUNDS

A COP'S JOURNEY
OF FAITH
THROUGH THE DARKNESS
OF PTSD

NICHOLAS ANTHONY

Nicholas Anthony
www.officernicholasanthony.com
invisawounds34@gmail.com

ISBN (print): 978-1-7351561-0-1
ISBN (e-book): 978-1-7351561-1-8
Library of Congress Number 2020910333

WARNING!

This book contains stories which capture the graphic and violent nature of police work and it depicts some of the struggles of the author suffering from post-traumatic stress disorder (PTSD) from traumatic events of police work. Some of the material in this book may be unsuitable for young readers. This includes anyone who is sensitive to or may be disturbed by stories of a graphic nature. Reader discretion is strongly advised.

Disclaimers:

This book contains my personal religious views as it relates to my struggles with PTSD. Those suffering from any suspected or diagnosed mental health disorders and/or symptoms should always seek out help from a qualified medical professional.

This book consists of a collection of real-life police incidents and circumstances that I have experienced as police officer in the course of my duties. The stories, conversations, and circumstances are based from my opinion and my best recollection of events over a period of time and are therefore not perfect. In addition, specific details and information contained herein may have been omitted, condensed, and/or altered, not limited to names, genders, location, physical descriptions, conversations, and circumstances, in order to fill in the gaps in my memory and/or protect the identities of those involved. In some case, two or more individuals have been combined into one character. Oh yeah, and all suspects are innocent until proven guilty.

This book reflects my personal opinions of police work, my department, and individuals as how I experienced them and is not representative in any way of all police officers, police departments, and/or affiliated local or federal government bodies.

DEDICATION

This book is dedicated to my two beautiful girls,
Aliana Rose and Daniella Marie.

May you grow each day with God and grace,
always seeking the Lord.

The people who walk in darkness
will see a great light. For those who
live in a land of deep darkness, a
light will shine.

Isaiah 9:2

CONTENTS

My heart starts rapidly pounding, and my vision is suddenly narrowing. I'm trying to focus on getting dressed. My peripheral vision is fading and blurry. My chest is feeling tight. With each breath is sharp pain, which travels up my chest into my neck. I feel like the world is closing in, and this sudden weight and pressure building and weighing down on me. I'm fighting the feeling of paranoia in my mind of being suddenly confined and somehow dizzy at the same time. I try to ignore the feeling as I'm getting dressed, and the normal locker room banter from the other guys is the room just muffled and overshadowed by the sound and feeling of my pounding heart.

I sit down in my usual spot in roll call, and while the sergeant was speaking, I have this urge to just scream from inside me, as I'm so uncomfortable. Normally after the sergeant finishes his brief, we usually sit around and talk for a few minutes before we have to drag ourselves up to get ready and load our cars for the day.

I ask the sergeant if he's done and then quickly run outside, trying to go about my day and load my cruiser, hoping the feeling will just subside. I begin driving down the road, but the feeling is building inside me. I'm trying to put it aside, but it is rapidly overcoming me. I pull into an empty parking lot behind a building and immediately start crying and gasping for air.

PREFACE

As police officers, we have a very real problem. We don't recognize how what we see, hear, smell, taste, and feel affects us on a daily basis. Our responses to violence and trauma are so subtle and long term that we do not realize what is happening to us until we begin to lose what is most important in our lives: our families, friends, health, spirituality, honor commitment, and sense of self-worth. We identify who we are by what we do, and when that begins to unravel, it can shake us to our core. The reality of those individuals who develop post-traumatic stress disorder is a harrowing and horrific real-life horror movie for most. A movie that doesn't end and continues to play is a perpetual, never-ending loop. The perils of serving as a member of the military are great, as are those of the first responder in law enforcement. Unimaginable amounts of trauma and stress are experienced by both. The issues of PTSD and operational stress-related injuries that, in the last few years, have led to the number one cause of death of police officers in our nation today, which is suicide.

The story you will encounter in this book is the author's journey while serving in both military and police functions and how the collective and combined experiences of those journeys took him through uncharted stormy seas he was not prepared to navigate through. Through firsthand raw experiences, you will learn of the continual trials and tribulations leading to pivotal moments of the author's experiences that set in motion a series of events that appeared seemingly improbable, unrecoverable, and would cause the average person to give up all hope. However, God had a different plan for Officer Nicholas Anthony by turning

1

a tragedy into a triumph. In defeating an invisible enemy, and being able to use his story as life raft to those losing the ability to continue to tread water in a raging sea of trauma and stress.

Invisible Wounds provides an accurate description of the struggle many police officers will deal with, all too many times on their own without any assistance from others. This book's value is not limited to those in policing, but to all emergency services personnel as well as family members of those suffering from PTSD. The author is a well-experienced police officer who had the courage to tell others not only something that is his story, but is also the stories of hundreds of other men and women who are the walking wounded in which their very real scars cannot be seen. Civilians and the general public will also be able to gleam valuable insight from this book and learn how life really is for those on the other side of the Blue Wall.

As a former law enforcement officer of fourteen years, a military veteran, and well-known expert and educator in the field of trauma intervention and education, I cite this book, Invisible Wounds, as an excellent resource that can contribute the resilience possible in all of us that sometimes seems unattainable. Hope and healing are available for all police officers struggling with the issues of trauma and stress, and God has the ability to unscramble any eggs. It is my prayer that this inspiring book will assist law enforcement, their family members, emergency services personnel, veterans, and the general public in their own journey of negotiating the unchartered waters of traumatic stress.

—**Dr. Robert L. Perkin**s, C.P. B.C.E.T.S., Chief of Chaplains,
California Practical Chaplain Association Member;
Board of Directors, Ontario Critical Incident Stress Foundation;
Professor, Applied Psychophysiology

INTRODUCTION

WALKING THROUGH THE VALLEY OF DARKNESS

When I began this book, I was writing from a place of uncertainty. My fate is continually evolving at God's hands. I want to assure you that although there will be some negative moments illustrated in this book, I have started to receive a positive outcome in the Spirit and my faith, which I think you will see that toward the end of this book. This book was written during some of the hardest times in my life with post-trauma stress disorder (PTSD). One thing I learned about PTSD is it can be like a roller coaster—at times you can have good moments; you can also have bad moments. During this process I had to navigate through the darkness in order to begin to see some light. While all of us may at some point walk through darkness, we will always find some source of light, no matter how small that light may appear at first. They say that "even the smallest light shines in the darkness." It is that light—no matter how small initially—we must cling to. John 1:5 tells us that the light that shines in the darkness cannot be overcome. If we believe God is light, then we must continue to press on forward toward him.

Writing this book started as a form of therapy for me, both mentally and spiritually, even up to present day, I continue forward on my journey discovering Jesus, like most Christians, being strengthened in the Spirit, and awaiting my destiny. My psychiatrist and psychotherapist have affirmed that writing things down is a form of therapy, even though it's been painful at times relive some of these events.

I have faith that I am becoming a new person, with a new mission and outlook on life. I pray that this book will serve as roadmap to recovery for others who are struggling with the darkness in which police officers and first responders find themselves on a daily basis. I hope this book will also bring much-needed awareness of PTSD among first responders. First responders are committing suicide across the country with over five recent incidents in my area alone in the last year of writing this. One thing I've learned so far in my struggle is this: There isn't enough being done to protect and take care of our first responders.

We aware of the issues surrounding military veterans as it concerns to PTSD; however, many people forget the countless people defending and serving us at home around the clock. The process of helping responders with PTSD is treated as an insurance claim and often involves municipalities fighting to dispute claims to avoid paying for compensation and treatment. Oftentimes, suffering responders will have to go without pay while they the process gets tied up in legal proceedings, further victimizing the individual. It is for this very reason I have personally discovered why most responders chose not to seek help until it is too late.

The uniform does not make you untouchable. Members of my own department have seen their fair share of officers assaulted and injured. A few years ago, we had an officer get attacked walking up a suspect's driveway, and he was pushed backward into an empty engine bay of a repair car in the driveway while the suspect continued to strike him. More recently, two of our officers (one male and one female) responded to a residence for an individual who was out of control. During the struggle, the suspect punched the male officer in the face, then picked the female officer up over his head and attempted to throw her off of the second-story deck. I have also been kicked, pushed, spit at, and on the other side of a baseball bat, knife, or another object with an angry person ready to use it.

Police officers are the first line of defense for this country. The first call is always to 911, whether it be for a car accident, or terrorist attack such as September 11, 2001. First responders are given this title because we are always the first people on scene. A police officer's job description on paper often fails to encompass everything an officer does. What I have found in my twelve years of law enforcement is that most people truly do not understand what we do day in and day out. Most people are under the impression that "nothing ever happens where I live," and so they stay in their bubble of comfort, going to and from work, mostly likely never needing police services except for minor auto accidents and stolen bicycles.

I hope that through this book, I am able to enlighten some people of the pains and stresses associated with job and the negative culture and darkness that surround cops both among co-workers and on the streets. I have learned that it is difficult to be a good Christian in this job. I have always believed in God, but as I began writing this book, I was on leave from work due to PTSD, and my struggle has exposed the evil within in myself and is pushing me to pursue God even more. I battled spiritually for the first few months while on leave and continued to battle daily, reading Scripture applying it to my current situation and my past.

I questioned God and his existence through this journey more than ever before. Yet I continued to stay the course and push through thoughts of doubt as signs of growth and progression. I found it strange that as I repented for certain actions and aspects in my life, at times I felt like I was even more under attack by darkness and temptation. I took this as a good sign that the "enemy" was worried he was losing me, but I knew I would prevail. A voice kept telling me, *Keep going, don't stray. You're doing so well.* And I will continue to hold on to this voice through this journey.

Throughout this book, I will add relevant scriptures here and there as they relate to my story.

Let's now begin this journey with a prayer:

Lord Jesus, forgive me for my sins of the past, forgive me for times of doubt, and give me the courage to continue in your path that you have destined for me. Although I live in uncertainty of my future, I thank you for this opportunity and know you will do all things for good. Lord, anoint this book. Give me the power of the Holy Spirit to organize my thoughts and words, for I am not a professional writer, but the words will nonetheless flow with divine anointing from my mind and hands. I pray that this book may be used to draw awareness about the issue of PTSD for first responders and that it may serve as a light in a world of darkness, in Jesus' name, Amen.

* * * * *

PART I

* * * * *

INVISIBLE WOUNDS

CHAPTER 1

A WARRIOR'S CALLING: ALL IN GOD'S PLAN

We can make our plans, but the Lord determines our steps.

PROVERBS 16:9

I can't say that I always wanted to be a police officer. I met many people in the academy who expressed that this was their childhood dream. Interestingly enough, some of these men and women were now older and at the cutoff in age for the academy, having been in another career all their lives. These individuals wanted to live their dream despite taking pay cuts from their regular civilian jobs. I, on the other hand, came about this job at a young age. I was in my last semester of my senior year of college when I was hired by my agency. Prior to that semester, becoming a police officer was really not on my radar. It was really only through my experience in the military that I became to be a civilian police officer.

I blame the Navy Seals really; I always was intrigued by special forces groups growing up as a child. I had every color picture book you can imagine about Navy Seals, Marines, Green Berets, and Delta Force. I watched *Navy Seals* the movie and drooled over documentaries with special operations folks crawling up the side of ship at sea at night and silently sneaking around with weapons drawn. I wanted to be one of these people more than anything. I loved all things military and tactical. My father, a US Army Reserve officer at the time, would return home from his annual trainings with teddy bears decked in Army battle dress uniforms and boots. To this day, "Sgt. Teddy" as I named him as a child, still sits upstairs in my bedroom. He lost his hat and shoes over the years, but his presence is a reminder of my path in this world.

As I grew a little older in my elementary school years, I had discovered my father's Army duffle bag in the basement one day full of all his old uniforms and gear (note to self: *Hide from kids*). My friend and I would dress up in his uniforms and gear, which never fit us, and I would ask my mother to make frequent trips to the local Army-Navy store to buy face camo paint, dog tags, and other military equipment. We would sneak around the backyards of our neighbors with painted camo faces and into the woods by our school. We would have little wars and fight about who got shot and who won the battle that occasionally ended some childhood friendships. One of my friends' fathers was a retired Marine veteran; my friend also later became a Marine and now is a police officer in another department. Another one of my friends in my group joined the Marines as well out of high school. He became a disgruntled veteran who is doing who knows what now; I lost touch with him. I remember one day talking to my friend's mother, who said, "There must have been something in the water" when we were born to make us all want to go into the service.

My path was slightly different from my friend's. While they went straight into the military, I was college bound, as my father had wanted. Insistent that I go to college, he told me that I could do Army ROTC (Reserve Officers' Training Corps) while in college and come out of it as a commission officer, unlike my enlisted friends. This was also the path he had taken while in college, mainly as a means to pay for his education. I attended Roger Williams University, which happened to have an Army ROTC program through the University of Rhode Island. ROTC is not like the junior programs you hear about in high school to help kids. Real Army ROTC is part of the US Army Reserves, and it is to this day one of the main commissioning sources in the country for Army officers.

The first two years of ROTC were without any commitment or obligation; the start of your junior year in the program was when you had to sign a contract. To get the full experience, I dove right in, attending PT (physical training) every Monday, Wednesday, and Friday at six o'clock in the morning. This was always led by the senior cadets and in the beginning resulted in my vomiting after every session. To this day, this was some of the hardest PT I have ever done. We took pride in the fact that our PT was brutal. We would get pounded in the gym with push-ups, sit-ups, burpees, and other forms of torture, then go for a run in the dark around the campus while regular students were still fast asleep sleep. When I first started, I would fall behind a lot. Master Sgt. Johnson, one of our instructors, would come and run next to me, encouraging me with comical and insulting, yet motivating, sayyings. Eventually I adapted, and as time when on, we took pleasure in new people trying out and vomiting on the ground during and after a PT session. We were the toughest group on campus—no other sports team came even close to the physical training sessions we did—and I began to enjoy it. I had a great sense of satisfaction as I showered in the locker room afterward, knowing everything I already accomplished before the first class. Even some of the teachers had respect for us, seeing us training as they would pull into the parking lot in the early-morning darkness.

I loved everything about the ROTC culture. I liked wearing a uniform around campus and being distinguished as a cadet. Wearing a uniform does something to you when you put it on—it makes you carry yourself differently. I believe you tend to hold yourself up higher and present more professionally when you wear a uniform, or at least that is how I always felt. On weekends we would often travel to a reserve training area somewhere and spend the weekend doing drills, obstacle courses, or simulated combat missions.

I remember the first time, though, that I questioned life as a soldier. We were participating in a joint field training exercise (FTX) with cadets from two other regional universities' ROTC programs. First, we exited the bus and geared up for our mission. Then, carrying M16 rifles and loaded rucksacks, we began a tactical road march into the woods for the weekend. That night, as we were setting up our patrol base, where we would sleep, I laid out my old-school military issue sleeping bag, which at the time did not have any outer waterproofing layer. I chose a spot between a large boulder and a tree. That night it began pouring down rain, like angry pouring, and I woke up in a river of water in a saturated sleeping bag. It was soon my time to be up to provide security on our perimeter anyway, but I was not alone. Pretty much everyone was up. It rained all through the night, and temperatures dropped as I eagerly awaited the sun's arrival. That morning, soaked and freezing, we scraped frozen camo sticks across our face, lighting them with matches to try to make them easier to apply. I was exhausted, I was cold, and I was absolutely miserable. At that moment, I questioned if this was what I wanted to do, but I did not let it dissuade me.

When we returned to campus after the long weekend, there was a great sense of accomplishment among the cadets as we went to the school cafeteria in our uniforms, our faces still covered in face camo and our uniforms rain drenched and reeking of sweat.

The following year, I enlisted in the US Army National Guard, under a program that would allow me to drill with a National Guard reserve unit while still being a member of ROTC. A lot of cadets chose to do this for both bragging rights and the personal experience. Some used this opportunity to attend enlisted basic training as well during their summer off from college. I told the recruiter I had wanted to be in an infantry unit; however, that unit was already chock-full of cadets, so the recruiter recommended the military police. At the time, I really did not have a desire to become a cop after the military and intended on making active duty a career. "Military Police are next best thing to infantry," said the recruiter. "They are pretty much infantry with Humvees." I was assigned to a military police unit under cadet status and was told I did not have to attend basic training because I was in ROTC and had already completed the first two years. A glutton for punishment, I had the summer off and wanted to stay in shape and told the recruiter I would like to go anyway, just for fun.

I was assigned a basic training ship day at the beginning of summer with plenty of time to return home for the start of my junior year of college. When I told my mom my plans, she did what most mothers would do: get angry. First, she blamed my father. "YOU STARTED THIS!" she yelled at him. Next, she pleaded with me to reconsider going into the military and told me my father had wanted to get out of the Army when he married her and he couldn't. She insisted I might meet someone, fall in love, and be trapped in the same predicament, but I didn't care at that point—there was no talking me out of it.

I thought of an older man I had once met walking through an Army-Navy store, browsing through the uniforms on the racks. The old man said, rather sadly, that his biggest regret was never joining the military. I will always remember how depressing this image was of this man, now older, who clearly felt he had missed out on something. I made a decision not to be that person.

* * * * *

I arrived at basic training at Fort Knox, Kentucky, about midnight. We were greeting by the drill sergeant in typical fashion and brought into a hallway, where we were immediately stripped of our civilian clothes and possessions. Army PT shirts and shorts were handed out, as we had to pack all of our worldly clothes away, which were then abruptly taken and locked away. We then proceeded to inprocess all through the night and until the following night, going from line to line, building to building, receiving bed lines, making our beds, which ironically we would not get to sleep in until the following night. We were herded around like cattle, getting our heads shaved, receiving inoculations, seeing physicians and dentists. The whole process of being stripped of personal identity and assigned a line and roster number, like a cow going to slaughter, was very much robotic and dystopian in nature.

I recall sitting "nut to butt," straddling benches with my nose practically touching the back of the bald head of the guy in front of me, inside the vaccine clinic. Slightly amused by the whole experience, I remember thinking that everyone here signed up for this, and in some countries people have no choice but to go into the military once they turn a certain age.

I began to learn that some of the people here pretty much had not choice either because of the lives, or lack of, they were from. I met a lot of people from the middle of nowhere who had no opportunities, and the military was just what everyone from the area did to receive pay and medical care. For some of these folks, this was the first time they had ever visited a dentist. I remember watching many of these folks holding bloody rags and ice packs after having several teeth pulled during inprocessing—not exactly Comfy Dental, if you know what I mean.

While going through the first week, dubbed "reception week," I couldn't help but start to feel like I did not need to be there. I was an ROTC cadet with two years of experience already. While these other younger kids were studying simple things in their battle books, such as the order of ranks, I could already take apart and reassemble an M16. I started regretting my decision to go to basic training pretty much right away and was determined not to let the drill sergeants to find out that I was an ROTC cadet destined to become an officer. This would no doubt cause unwanted attention.

At the end of reception is when you are assigned to a section to begin your basic training. As we sat straddling our duffle bags on the blacktop between the barracks, the drill sergeants began calling off roster numbers of those who would "ship" and begin their basic training. Meanwhile, the rest of the poor folks remained in reception purgatory due to issues that were holding them behind. These issues could be anything from medical issues that arise during inprocessing or something as simple like there were no more boots left in your size. Either way you did not want to stay in reception, frozen in time.

Finally, the drill sergeant called my number, and I scrambled with everyone else to my ship area, logging around my two heavily stuffed duffle bags. Suddenly, as I sat down on my duffle bag, a screw on my glasses came out, and one of the ear pieces fell off. (Full disclosure: I am blind as a bat and pretty much useless without my contacts. They don't let you wear contacts in basic training due to the high risk of eye infection. The Army usually solves this problem by giving us vision-impaired folks a nice sturdy pair of Army-issue glasses humorously called BCGs or "birth control glasses." These glasses are so hideous that you will have zero chance with anyone of the opposite sex. Unfortunately I had not been issued my BCGs yet, and my frail mall specials decided to fail me at the absolute worst possible moment.) Sitting there, I frantically broke a piece of spiral from my battle book binding and somehow jerry-rigged the earpiece back on with it.

Sitting there, proud of my last-minute ingenuity, I was approached by a master sergeant who said he was the National Guard liaison on the base and that there was an issue that he needed to speak to me about and to tell the drill sergeant that I was not going to ship. The master sergeant then walked away and left me to the wolves to try to explain this to the next drill sergeant that called my number. My number was called again as they were loading everyone inside a cattle car. I attempted to approach the drill sergeant, who was calling the numbers, and efficiently tried to explain what this master sergeant had just told me. He immediately cut me off and screamed at me (which is what I expected) for attempting to talk to him. Other drill sergeants observed this and took the opportunity to swarm onto me for having the audacity to speak. (This is well known as a "shark attack" in military circles.) I immediately regretted my decision to approach him and decided to just go with the flow, thinking, They'll figure it out eventually. So I ran around for the next twenty to thirty minutes, just doing what I was told, when I was pulled aside and yelled at by the same drill sergeant, who by then was standing next to the master sergeant. It took everything in my power not to say, "I told you so," but I knew better.

As I start walking back with the master sergeant, a mostly pleasant fellow in comparison to the drill sergeants, he tells me there is a problem with the medical paperwork that came with me. When we arrive at his office, he asks me, "How did you get here? You don't have medical papers." I then go through my packet myself and show him the Department of Defense Medical Review Board physical that I received as an ROTC cadet. He looks at the paperwork and says, "What is this? Are you prior service?" At this point, I decide to tell him that I am an ROTC cadet attached to a National Guard unit under the new program and I chose to go to basic training to do something for the summer. He appears confused and tells me I might remain at reception for a prolonged period of time before the situation is rectified. At this point, I tell him that I do not need to complete enlisted basic training if I am going to get stuck here, because I am already in the ROTC program. The master sergeant makes a few phone calls to the ROTC command on base and back at my school and verifies this information. He then says, "Well, we're going to be sending you home then, good luck," and releases me back to the drill sergeants at reception.

I spent the next week and half or so sweeping stairs and cleaning barracks among other poor souls who have been in reception purgatory for several months awaiting the military's red tape to discharge them. I couldn't help but start to worry myself about how long I would be stuck there. There were some kids there who had been stuck in reception for several months.

I was sweeping the stairs one day when suddenly one of

the drill sergeants yells, "HEY, YOU WITH THE BROKEN GLASSES, GET OVER HERE!" I put down my broom and ran over to him, and he says, "So you're a college boy, huh? Going be an officer?" His next words brought a sigh of relief, as I started to panic that they had discovered my little secret: "You're lucky, Officer Boy. Looks like your heading home today." And before you knew it, they had me change, handed me bus tickets to the airport, and off I went.

As I landed back home, I had mixed feelings of relief and disappointed heading down the escalator with my shaven head and my mother and sister waiting at the bottom. I guess it just wasn't meant to be; sometimes we have to accept that divine intervention exists, and basic training was not in God's plan for me that summer.

CHAPTER 2

CADET LAND: WHERE BUTTER BARS ARE MADE

I can do all things through Christ who strengthens me.
PHILIPPIANS 4:13

The mystical land where ROTC and West Point cadets exist outside of the regular Army is humorously known as "cadet land" because the cadet, a foreign entity to the regular Army—not soldier and not yet officer—trains in this realm of quasi-military college life. ROTC cadets entering their senior year converge from all over the country, as well as folks in Officer Candidate School (OCS), in the epitome of cadet land known as the Leader Development Assessment Course (LDAC) or "Warrior Forge." This five-week training evaluates cadets and OCS candidates in various leadership positions in both garrison and field environments. Cadets will take a battery of tests (including a PT test, Combat Water Survival test, written and field land navigation tests), qualify on various weapons, and be evaluated on their ability to lead soldiers in a stressful environment.

The following summer, after being sent home from basic, I was rather excited to attend LDAC and complete it for my own sense of accomplishment. LDAC is a stressful time for a cadet, as you are being tested and ranked nationally against your peers and your success relies on your performance on various tasks.

In one of the main events, your land navigation test, you are required to set off on your own into the woods with a map and compass, plotting coordinates and finding points along the way in various terrain. To prove that you actually made it to these points, there was a paper punch with a different shape at each point that you had to mark your answer sheet with. For officers in training, land navigation is conducted both at night and day, and this is a pass-or-fail exercise you must complete without any assistance. Even if you run any other cadets along the way, you are forbidden to talk to them at all, and being caught would result in an immediate failure. The land navigation test is a requirement for graduation, and some cadets did not pass.

During my land navigation test, I got off to a good start. I stuck to the trails and would shoot azimuths from known points, then try to make my way back to the trails. This worked for my pretty well until I shot an azimuth and couldn't find the point I was looking for. I assumed I miscalculated and figured I would just turn around and walk back to the trail. Unfortunately, as I was heading back to the trail, I realized I should have reached it already. Suddenly, I became disoriented. I had no idea where the trail was or which direction to go, so I panicked. Fearing I would be lost out there, I dropped to my knees and began to pray for help when suddenly a cadet walked by. I immediately jumped up and silently gestured for help, then followed him back to the trail, where we both went our separate ways.

This training cumulates with an eight-day field training exercise meant to simulate a combat deployment to a fictitious country. It's a grueling week where you basically walk with a fifty-pound rucksack on for eight days straight days, running missions along the way. During one mission, we were even picked up by Blackhawk helicopters and flown to our next mission. This was a surreal experience, sitting with the door of the helicopter open while the pilots hugged the tree line. When we got to our destination, they gave us a countdown to time on target, the helicopters briefly touched town, and we had to scramble out and take a position laying behind our rucksacks, weapons drawn, to simulate landing in a hostile environment. This was probably the coolest thing I have ever done, lying there on the ground at that moment with the blades of the helicopter whishing violently overhead amid a mighty windstorm. My adrenaline was through the rough the roof as I watched several helicopters take off from the open field after dropping their troops.

Nighttime in the field was often interrupted by attacks, and as a means to further sleep-deprive you and keep you on your toes. After being attacked at night, you would have to pack up and find a new location to sleep in. During daytime patrols, moving from checkpoint to checkpoint, I would often find myself falling asleep whenever we stopped to take a knee without even realizing it, that is, until someone would knock me on my helmet when we started moving again.

On the eighth day you walk out of the woods and make the long trek back to the barracks, looking a lot like death itself. Stumbling down the last leg of the march, you reach the barracks-lined road filled with other regiments in various stages of LDAC. All the other cadets from other regiments line the road clapping and cheering you on, which is a rewarding experience; however, most of us were just too tired at that point to care. I just wanted a hot meal and shower because it had been a week without either.

I went to LDAC in June that summer, which was held on the other side of the country at Joint Base Lewis McCord in Washington State. After what had happened to me the previous summer, it felt good to complete something. You have to just take your circumstances how they are given to you sometimes.

When I got back to school, I was offered a scholarship through the National Guard to pay for the last two years of college. The stipulation was I could no longer go active duty and would be required to serve my obligation in the National Guard as an officer. This isn't exactly what I had wanted, but it was a hard offer to turn down. This ultimately brought me to start looking at police departments because I now needed a full-time job.

* * * * *

In more recent days, when my therapist asked me why I chose to become a cop, I explained that in my mind, being a police officer was a natural progression from the military world that I was used to. The military has a defined structure, and their personnel wear uniforms, as does the police world. Truth be told, I originally entered college as biology major, but I suck at math, or else I would have had greater aspirations in life. After I looked into being a cop, I realized the pay and benefits were decent in law enforcement. My father, on the other hand, was not happy with this career choice, saying I wasted my time going to college only to end up becoming a cop. Nevertheless, I applied to several departments my senior year in college, and three of them were looking to hire me or place me on a waiting list the next time they were hiring. Only one of the departments was sending anyone to the next police academy. I ended up accepting their offer based solely on this. I didn't really care about the town dynamics, individual pay, or benefits offered—I just wanted a job.

Around the same time, I had met Francesca, a nursing student in her second year at a nearby college. We feel in love, of course, and at the end of the year, she and my family watched me receive my commission as an Army officer. The same day of college graduation, later in the afternoon, I traded my cap and gown for an Army dress blue uniform. Along with my fellow new officers, I my raised my right hand, swearing in and receiving my ceremonious first salute from one of the sergeant instructors, who we now magically outranked. Standing there proudly, my father, a former Army officer himself, pinned my new shiny gold 2nd lieutenant "butter bars" on my uniform. I continued on in the National Guard one weekend a month, plus two weeks a year, for another four years while also working as a police officer at the same time.

A year or so after I had been on the department, I was required to go for more active duty training as required of all new Army officers. This training is part of a new officer's career and was previous known as Officer Basic Course or OBC for short. At the time, it was known as Basic Officer's Leadership Course, or BOLC, and was divided into phases. Phase I consisted of your commissioning source, which for me was ROTC. Phase II was part of a new program to train all Army officers regardless of their job specialty to receive additional combat training focused on the current theater of operations (Iraq and Afghanistan). I started my phase II in September and drove with my father to assigned training location, which was Fort Sill, Oklahoma.

While driving across the country, my father and I comically made note of the redundant scenery on the side of road that stretches through most of the interior of the country—corn, lots of it. Every state we went through, we joked about being greeted by corn lining the sides of the road. When we got to Oklahoma, my father flew back home and I drove onto the base and headed to the assigned area for check-in. The barracks were unlike that of any other training I had been to and consisted separate rooms with three to four beds each off of a hallway. This was a nice change from the open bay layout.

I took to one of my roommates almost instantly, as we were both from the Northeast. He and I were in the same squad, and on leave we would always go to restaurants in the town around the base and occasionally made the trip to Oklahoma City, where we toured the bombing memorial, and other spots like the Cowboy Museum and Bricktown. We ate a famous steak house in the area that had a cattle yard literally in the back of the restaurant. Others in our platoon would joke about how we were like a married couple. During our stay at Fort Sill we had found a local cigar shop not far from the base. The owner there would make us designer coffees and lattes and allow us in the back member lounge to hang out. We were there all the time, and we frequently brought other people from our platoon as well, which I'm sure they appreciated.

Intrigued by all the sweet-smelling pipe tobacco of different varieties and "flavors," we decided to buy ourselves pipes and would sit there continuously puffing away on weekends that we had off. It took some practice, though, as there seems to be an art form to keeping a pipe lit.

BOLC phase II was an interesting course in deed. Made up all newly ordained lieutenants, from ROTC, West Point, and OCS, we outranked our instructors, which made for things to be very awkward. They consisted a group of disgruntled sergeants who were in between deployments and probably did something wrong to be there. Either way, it appeared they were not happy about their assignment to train a bunch of former college idiots.

The training started with a week of the new Army combative program. We rolled around, fighting each other and the cadre pretty much all day during the first week. We went to the range for basic and advanced rifle marksmanship. We were issued all the latest gear being fielded overseas to include night vision goggles that attached to our helmets and these really cool infrared laser/lights, know as a PEQ-2, on our M4 rifles. This was a far cry from the old-school M16A2 "muskets" we were trained on previously. We did night shooting, shooting from vehicles, and a lot of urban combat training.

Fort Sill has an area called Liberty City that is set up just for urban combat training. At the end of the training, we "deployed" to a forward operating base a few miles outside Liberty City for a week or two and ran twenty-four hour operations in and out of city in simulated combat missions. We shot both blank rounds and marking cartridge rounds out of our M4s. The instructors would light off "artillery simulators," which are basically controlled explosive devices to simulate grenades and mortar rounds going off around you. This training culminated with a long-distance ruck march back to our barracks. There was no welcoming committee this time, though, or clapping for that matter. Instead our training company all but put the entire base of Fort Sill on lockdown for a missing GPS "plugger." These items consist of sensitive military technology, and losing one is a big deal. The instructors made us empty all of our gear on the front lawn of the barracks. After being threatened various times by the instructors that we would be out there all night, our rooms and personal bags were searched to no avail. Wouldn't you know it, the unit somehow ended up in an instructor's personal vehicle. I'm pretty sure that he forgot that he had it all along, and they never apologized for accusing us of course.

After graduating BOLC phase II, you were granted leave for two weeks before you had to return to your next active duty station, which for me was Fort Leonard Wood, Missouri. I couldn't wait to go fly home. I drove to the airport in Oklahoma, left my car there, and flew home for leave. After leave was over, I flew back to Oklahoma to pick up my car and drove to Missouri to check in for BOLC phase III.

BOLC phase III is your job specific training or what we call your MOS (military occupational specialty). Being from a National Guard military police unit, I was guaranteed placement as an MP (military police offer). One thing about MP BOLC that struck me off the bat was how well it was run in comparison to BOLC II. The main instructors consisted of two captains with several deployments as both platoon leaders and company commanders under their belt. We also had a well-experienced staff sergeant too.

There is a lot of prestige in being military police officer. I can't speak for other branches, but Army MPs truly do it all. People often joke that MP is short for "multipurpose," and this is so true of Army MPs, who have morphed from their original role in the past of law enforcement to combat troops. While other military branches maintain this policing type of work, most Army installations now are guarded by Department of Defense Police. The MP mission has drastically changed since the war in the Middle East. Iraq and Afghanistan were undergoing structural changes post invasion, and this included the reorganization and training of the indigenous police forces. Police in Iraq are very different than police elsewhere; this is a combat zone, and their job includes fending off insurgents more than giving tickets. What better group of people than the MPs to embed with local Iraqi police to train and fight alongside them.

Army MPs where one of the main specialties used post invasion in Iraq for recovery operations so much so that other Army units, such as Field Artillery, were actually trained and converted into MPs units because the need was great.

MP BOLC was a well-oiled machine. The main captain in charge was an ex-Norte Dame football player, rugged and tough, and he demanded respect from everyone. The captain held everyone to high standards, and he would rip you a new one if you did not approach him with respect. Fortunately he liked me, and I knew how not to piss him off, but it was amazing how juvenile some of the other people in the class were at times. For instance, one guy was caught writing stupid sayings inside of portable toilet with a permanent marker. He spent the rest of the day inside of it, cleaning the whole thing top to bottom, and they nearly expelled him from the class.

MP BOLC ran into the winter months for my class, and we spent a lot of time doing convoy operation trainings, urban combat, and room clearing in the mock Iraqi city they had on base. We participated in the German Armed Forces Badge Proficiency test, which I was assigned to run for one of my evaluations. I had to coordinate with the German Army Captain Liaison we had on base, which was pretty cool considering I got to talk to someone from another country's military. The GAFB consists of different events you have to pass to earn the badges, which you can wear on your dress uniform. The worst part of the GAFB was a twelve-kilometer ruck march with a minimum required thirty-five-pound pack.

This day sucked. After I turned around at the halfway point, I could already feel my feet swelling in my boots as sweat and blood soaked my socks. I was in so much pain on the way back, I decided to run/limp the rest of the way in an effort to make the pain end quicker. People driving by on the post were beeping and cheering me on because they probably saw the agony in my face. When I got back to my room afterward, my feet were a mess. I could barely get my boots off, and the tips of my socks were blood stained. The bottoms of both my soles were one large white deflated bubble that already popped and oozed puss. My heel on one foot pretty much had a hole in. I tried to walk into the shower on the sides of my feet. I approached the shower and put all of my weight on the towel handle to try to alleviate any pressure on my feet while entered the shower, but the towel rack wasn't having it. It snapped off the wall, and I fell right into the shower. Needless to say, I was not able to get the GAFB badge.

Thanksgiving came while I was away, and we were granted leave for the holiday weekend. I was still dating Francesca at the time, and she flew out to St. Louis to meet me. We stayed at a nice downtown hotel and were the only two people in there in the hotel restaurant having Thanksgiving dinner, but they treated us good and gave us plenty of food. Francesca and I got to go up in the St. Louis Arch, visit the local zoo, and even see the Thanksgiving Day Parade in front of the hotel. It was a nice break from the training and a nice way to make the best out of a holiday away.

MP BOLC ended much like every other training with a mock deployment that lasted a week or longer in the field; however, this time it was in the middle of January with an average of fifteen degrees out. I think I wore every single piece of clothing I was issued in layers to try to stay warm. We ran simulated missions to the mock city at all hours of the day and night. The instructors constantly were lobbing CS (tear gas) grenades at us, and it seemed they had a never-ending supply of them at their disposal. Dawning gas masks and running through CS fog, we stormed buildings, carried our "wounded" over our shoulders, and seized areas of the city. It was all very much fun, and I absolutely loved this stuff, minus choking on CS gas.

The day after graduation, during outprocessing, we had to turn all our equipment in for inspection. The civilian employees at the Central Issuing Facilities (CIF) where your turn in your gear are notoriously miserable, and I swear they take enjoyment out of refusing gear back for not being clean and other things. One miserable woman refused to take one of my canteens back because it had "moisture" in it. Now, I had emptied both my canteens a week prior, and they had been drying upside in my room since. The worst part is, you can't leave base and go home until you clear CIF. She tells me to come back another time when my canteen is dry. I was so mad because this was literally the only thing preventing me from going home. I bought a brand-new canteen on base, went right back a few minutes later, then handed it to her with the tag still on it. "Here you go!" I said.

Being on active duty, even if it was only a half of a year, was a good experience—it makes you appreciate life on a military instillation. After graduation, I drove home, determined to make it to back East from Missouri in one shot. I made it to New Jersey in one stretch and would have arrived home according to my GPS at 10:30 p.m., but I was beat and stopped at a hotel. I went to the Irish bar next door and had a Ruben sandwich, then called it a night. The next morning I drove home.

* * * * *

When I returned home, a few years went by, and I eventually got married to Francesca. Then we bought a house together, bringing my mother's earlier premonitions into play. At this point, I had been in the National Guard for six years total and would have to do four more according to my obligation. Normally National Guard and Reserve soldiers only have to do six years total, but because I had the scholarship for college, they wanted me to serve an additional four more years. Along with the stresses of police life, I faced problems with evil in my guard unit in the form of another tyrannical officer. Hungry for power, he often treated me and the rest of some of the command staff like crap, and life was miserable both at my regular job as a cop and at weekend drill. I wanted out of the military. I had not yet deployed, but I had also lost all interest in deploying overseas, being newly married. I worried what a deployment would look like in a deployment with him and could foresee problems with him maybe trying to pin his mistakes on me.

We were approaching our annual two-week training one year when I received a phone call from the readiness sergeant at my National Guard Unit.

"Hey, you're allergic to nuts?" he asked in surprise.

"Yeah," I said. "Why?"

"I don't think it's going to be a big deal," he said. "You're going to need to go to the medical detachment and at least get a medical alert tag."

The weird part was, during six years in the military, I'd been through physicals and medical inprocessing at active duty trainings, yet no one had ever asked me about my allergy to tree nuts. Inside my medical folder from day 1, on the first page, highlighted in green and bold letters, were the words, "ALLERGY TO TREE

NUTS."

I went to the medical detachment and spoke with the doctor and was basically told I was going to be placed on certain limitations and I could not be deployed due to my condition. The doctor tells me that emergency medical treatment is remote in Afghanistan, and as an officer, I might have to dine with several of the local indigenous leaders and eat their food. "It's possible you could eat something that has nuts in it," he explained. "The nearest hospital could be hours away on a helicopter and you won't make it." He then asked me how I managed all these years in the military with eating the MREs (meal(s) ready to eat), which sometimes contain nuts.

"Easy," I said, "I just did not eat the stuff with nuts in it."

"Well," he says, "we would hate to have to explain to your family that you died from eating a nut in Afghanistan. I'm sorry."

I left there thinking, OK, so that's not the worst news. In fact, it's really not that bad.

A few weeks later, I received a letter from the National Guard Bureau, telling me I was no longer qualified for military serve and would be given an honorable discharge. I felt the timing was right, even though I did not fulfill my entire obligation; I still served six years in total.

I had to think that God was in control of this whole situation and wanted me out for some reason. I later learned that a month after I was discharged, my unit went to their annual training, and a lot of bad things went down in those two weeks. I was told that the other officer I mentioned earlier ended up being investigated after some incidents there, and he was eventually pulled from his position of leading soldiers and placed somewhere else. The next year my unit deployed to Afghanistan, and a vehicle housing explosives drove into the front gate, where some of my unit's soldiers were injured.

I'm not sure why I was discharged so abruptly or if there was a reason behind it. Maybe I would have developed PTSD much earlier. Either way, God must have been in control of everything and so ended my time in the military. What is interesting, however, was that he did not prevent me from going into the military and allowed that happen. God gives us free will, but at the end of the day, if he has other plans for us, he will ultimately guide us with his hand.

CHAPTER 3

THE POLICE ACADEMY: THE PATH TO THE BADGE

Praise the Lord, who is my rock. He trains my hands
for war and gives my fingers skill for battle.
PSALM 144:1-2

After applying to various police departments and being hired by my agency, I had received a letter of instructions from the police academy. The letter instructed recruits to arrive on time, wearing a suit and tie, with their issued academy uniforms on a hanger. The letter then stated that recruits must park in the first row of parking next to one another and wait in their vehicles for further instructions.

As I sat there waiting in my vehicle, one by one various state troopers and police officers from around the state came out and began removing recruits from their vehicles. From inside my vehicle, I awaited my fate as I watch students before me standing at attention in the front of their vehicles while officers screamed at them and ripped through their cars, tossing their personal belongings all over the ground. Soon enough it was my turn, but I'd been tipped off by someone from the previous academy to clean my car out beforehand. While others' personal belongings and trash began to pile up next to their cars on the ground, the instructors were lucky if they even found a penny in my car. The instructor, a very large-looking state trooper, had me stand at my front bumper, opened my door, and in shock found a spotless and empty interior. He walked around my car (which had just been washed too) looking for something wrong when he stopped at some sticker residue on the back window. Just days before, I had removed the military police sticker on my back window to avoid unwanted attention but couldn't get all the sticker residue off. The instructor then demanded to know what I had removed from the vehicle. Determined to give as little information as possible, I replied, "A military-related sticker." Unfortunately, I just gave him all the information he needed.

"Oooh, so you were in the military?" he bellows. "So you think this is a joke, huh? You think you're just going to breeze your way through this and not help your buddies out, huh?"

While being pestered, I could see out of the corner of my eye other recruits doing jumping jacks and push-ups in their rigid dress suits next to me. Others were being screamed at while they frantically tried to clean up the piles of trash and belongings that were ripped out of their cars.

We were then rushed inside to locker room, where we had an unreasonable amount of time to get into our academy uniforms. Being from the military, I knew the game that was being played and knew this was an unwinnable game. "READY, MOVE!" the instructor would yell after time was up, and we would all scramble to the tape line, half dressed, with some in their underwear and crooked neckties. After certain and predicable failure, we were told to get back into our personal suits, again under a time hack you couldn't make. This continued for a long time: changing back and forth from our academy uniforms to our suits—not until we succeeded, but until they decided they were done torturing us. Then came drill and ceremony (marching) in the parking lot for what seemed like forever while we were continuously yelled at. The first day lasted until sometime late at night. I was exhausted and thought, This is going to suck a lot worse than I thought.

The rest of the first week followed suit. On cue, every morning we would line up in the gym, and someone would have forgotten to lock their locker. The instructors would walk out of the locker room holding a pile of some poor unfortunate soul's clothes and dump it on the floor in front of the class formation. Just like the military, when one screws up, we all screwed up, and so we would all pay for it with extra PT.

The idiot I am, I had decided not to fully prepare physically for the academy. Coming from all the military PT I was doing, I was tired of running every morning and figured taking a few months off before the academy wouldn't hurt. I immediately regretted this during the first weeks of the academy. "SOME OF YOU DID NOT PREPARE AT ALL, THOUGHT THIS WAS GOING TO BE A JOKE!" the instructor yells. Out of breath from countless push-ups, I could not agree with him and hate myself more.

The thing I remember most about the first few days of the academy was really all the negativity being preached about the job. I am not sure if they were trying to warn us, scare us, or make us quit, but I remember all different instructors telling us basically how much the job sucked. They showed us countless slides of dead and decomposing bodies, as well as fatal car accidents, and talked about how we would most likely change and lose relationships with friends and family. They talked about the long hours being stuck or held over on calls, going without eating, and the thanklessness of the job. They talked about the high divorce rate and how most of them and us will eventually be personally sued by citizens and subjected to lawsuits.

I could not help but get the sense that the instructors themselves were unhappy and bitter with the life they chose. It was all very depressing to be honest. I remember sitting there thinking, Geez, if it's that bad, why are we all here? Other recruits shared the same sentiment, but we mostly shrugged it off, as they were exaggerating and trying to scare us. Unfortunately, what I would discover later was that they were right. The pay and benefits are decent, but at what price?

* * * * *

The rest of the academy is spent both in classroom and abroad. We spent mornings doing PT or defensive tactics, rolling around in goose crap on the field. We followed up with pool sessions where we would swim in slacks and dress shirts to simulate swimming in a uniform. Pool sessions consisted of swimming laps, rescue drills, and a final test that required you to rescue a weighed dummy from a sunken car frame at the bottom of the pool. After lunch, you adorned your "Smurf" blue uniforms with your duty belt and trusty red plastic training gun. Afternoons were mostly classroom lecture, learning about topic such as report writing, search and seizure, and due process. You would learn about investigating traffic accidents and the differences between skids and yaw marks. We got certified in radar and visually estimating speed, a humorous process in which you have to successful guess the speed of passing cars within five miles above or below the radar speed.

At midpoint in the academy, you receive your real firearm from your department, which you are in entrusted with. One of the students in my academy, however, had to secure his firearm back at his department each day after the academy because a previous recruit from his department had killed himself with his during a previous academy. I'm not sure what the reasons were behind the suicide, but it's sad nonetheless.

The range weeks are probably one of the best times in the academy, because you get some fresh air outside of the classroom. The first day of range week began like this: "Who has never shot a gun before?" Surprisingly there were a few hands that went up, and what followed was a "the bullet comes out of this end" speech. Growing up with guns from early age and being in the military, I had no issues with the range, and later I became a firearms instructor myself at my own department, teaching other officers. This was something I was always passionate about and enjoyed.

At the range we would run an obstacles course, which involved climbing ropes, hopping over sections of fence, and crawling under barbed wire. Every day we ran a hill next to the range for PT in the mornings, which had an ungodly steep incline. We would also run down the main road outside of the range facility in view of the public while passersby would shout out, "Pigs!" In the end though, it was better than being stuck in the classroom learning about motor vehicle code and trying not to fall asleep.

Toward the end of the academy, we spent a week doing EVOC, or Emergency Vehicle Operations Course, and got to drive really fast and push the limits of our cruisers. Three students and an instructor would pile into a cruiser, and one student would drive a cone course while the rest of us would white-knuckle it in the back seat. The instructors, most likely on some sort of medication, would remain relatively calm even as we often lost control of the car. During one of my turns driving in the rain, I actually spun the cruiser off the course and ended up on the grass field next to the track. The instructor barely looked up from his clipboard and calmly asked me to start again. Among general fast driving, we learned the fastest way to take corners, tricks to avoid collisions, and pursing vehicles. You would be surprised how fast fifty miles per hour feels when you're swerving back and forth between cones placed only a short distance apart.

After EVOC is over, the remainder of the academy is spent doing your "test outs" for PT, then defensive tactics, followed by a week of role-playing. Testing out for PT meant scoring a certain percentage better than your initial score at the start of the academy. Defensive tactics concluded with being hosed in the face with OC (oleoresin capsicum), a type of pepper spray that is just horrible—like the devil himself spit in your face.

The best way I can describe it is that your entire face feels like it has been lite on fire, then with burning sand in your eyes you have to blindly fight and handcuff an instructor. Immediately after completing this task, the adrenaline wears off and the pain some-how doubles in intensity. Unable to open your eyes, they drag you over to garden hose and drench your face with flowing water. This immediately gives you relief with a cool refreshing blast until the second you remove the hose and the heat surges right back, some-how feeling much worse than before. As more and more recruits finish, the line at the hose piles up with choking, orange-stained recruits clawing at the one hose for a brief moment of relief.

Eventually you have to take yourself away from the hose, as the water actually does reactivate the OC. The best thing to do is to get the wind in your face to dry it up. For some reason, while walking around after being sprayed, you have the sudden urge to rip your shirt off, which is mostly likely still covered in OC, thus the parade of now orange-faced, shirtless recruits pacing around and gagging.

Culminating the end of defensive tactics test out is "ground zero," which is probably the most difficult experience in the academy. This event has varied from class to class but usually consists of some means to completely tire you out by doing a series of strenuous tasks and events for a long period of time and then having you fight and subdue several instructors by yourself. Instructors hold nothing back during ground zero and bare fist are thrown at you, whether you are a guy or gal, and you better defend yourself or you will catch one or a few to the face. Wearing zero protective head gear or gloves, we had to go through a gauntlet of being attacked by various sides and crowded by others. Both standing and on your knees, you were wailed at with heavy foam strike bags while being kicked by people's feet. Following different stations, you tire very quickly and start catching bags in the face, jarring you and even splitting open skin on several recruits' heads. After being abused for some time and now exhausted, a timer begins and you have to subdue three different instructors one at time. Completely out of breath, you see the well-rested instructor come out swinging and you must try to use the proper control tactics to subdue them. During my ground zero, I was determined to subdue each instructor as fast as I could because I knew the longer I was in there, the more tired I would get. My strategy was making it through fast, hard, and quick. I figured by mustering what little energy I had, I would get the job done quickly, because endurance would ultimately fail you in this situation.

My strategy actually worked—I went extremely hard and took care of the first two guys very quickly. The last instructor came out and pretended to be compliant right away. "OK, Officer,

I give up. What do you want me to do?"

I should have foreseen this as a trick, but I figured it was worth a shot. Being the Italian I am, I talk with my hands, and I began to tell him to put his hands behind his back. Of course as I am explaining this, I physically lift up both of my hands in Italian sign language to demonstrate for him, and I opened up a clear shot for him.

It happened so quick, I really never even saw it coming, I just felt the blow, saw stars, and moments later tasted the warm metallic liquid pooling in my lower lip. I raised my hand to my mouth, held out my hand, and looked down at the blood on my fingers. Now, according to witnesses I supposedly sounded a lot like Clint Eastwood in Dirty Harry. Filled with rage, I said to the instructor, "You cut me." Moments later, he was successfully subdued on the ground, then it took me somewhere around thirteen minutes to subdue all the three instructors. Thankfully I was one of the shortest completions, as other recruits had carried on much longer and began to lose steam, fighting the instructors.

Ground zero is no joke, and that night I felt very much like I had been hit by a train and violated by the conductor driving it at the same time. Sitting there with a fat lip, I concluded that ground zero served as a reminder of the worst-case situation. You could easily be tired from a pursuit or outnumbered in a bar and have to defend yourself and protect all the tools on your belt that could also be taken from you and used against you. This exercise is also a scary reminder of the reality of police work.

If you think no one is ever going to touch you on the streets, think again. Assaulting a police officer results in a slap on the wrist in most states—just another charge someone willing to commit crime does not mind adding to their list. In some case, it may even be a rite of passage to have this charge on you for status reasons when you go to prison.

The last weeks of the academy are spent doing role-playing and responding to fake domestic disturbances and calls for service. You and a partner drive around in a cruiser with a radio, and you are dispatched to a specific building for a call for service. Most of the things that happen in role-play are extreme, and the instructors like to up the ante for the pure joy of it. It's common in role-playing for the players to run away from you, steal your gun, or even take off in your cruiser because you forgot to lock the doors. The final event in role-playing consisted of a large disturbance in which all the players pile into a building and basically act crazy—throwing things at you, fighting, running from you, jumping on top of cruisers, and creating overall chaos. All of the recruits were dispatched to this call for the final scenario, and it was a complete disaster.

The following week you practice marching and looking good for graduation and all of your family and friends, but that's only is "if you graduate" according to one of the head instructors, who threatened us we wouldn't graduate even up until the morning of graduation. Overall my class started with thirty-six recruits, and three didn't make it. Not too bad, but it really isn't until after the academy that I think this job begins to weed people out. After graduation, it's on to your departments and into the darkness.

* * * * *

I sit here now writing this, feeling very much like a broken man and a shell of what I once was. I have been more afraid now than ever. I learned firsthand what *anxiety*, a word that previously had no meaning to me, feels like. The truth is, no academy can prepare you for this job. The academy is really just a formality, and one thing is for sure: It does not teach you how to be a cop.

CHAPTER 4

FROM ROOKIE <u>TO</u> VET: CYNICISM <u>AND</u> DISAPPOINTMENT

Wisdom lights up a person's face, softening its harshness.
ECCLESIASTES 8:1

All cops fall into cynicism and hardness. It comes with the territory sooner or later, but we don't start out that way. New cops are ready to save the world, one bad guy at a time, until the reality of policing hits. As time went on, however, toward the onset of my PTSD, I actually starting having even more compassion and empathy for people.

Rookie, rook, or boot are terms often used to refer to newbies at the department. Graduating the academy is a proud moment, but it is one that briefly ends as soon as you show up the first day at your department. The parties are over; you worked hard to get where you are now, and there you on your first day with an empty gun in your holster, standing at the back of roll call very awkwardly in the uniform you haven't earned yet. You quickly realize your value in the first few moments to the rest of the department as everyone that walks in the room looks at you for the first time. You don't dare take a seat, and you call everyone sir and ma'am regardless of rank.

I was lucky enough to graduate the academy with two other

recruits from my department, so in my case, I was not alone. As the mostly senior day shift officers walk in room, one of them asked us which one of us came out first place in the academy. Your performance in the academy on written tests determines your order of seniority among the other recruits at your department. I came in the middle of the other two guys, but we were only separated by one or two points from each other. Fortunately, that point or two made the difference between me going to second shift right away and my friend spending several years on midnights.

The same officer asked us each if we have ever been in a fight in our lives and whether we had won. I said, "Yeah, of course" (if you count elementary school). We were soon taken upstairs and introduced to our field training officers, or FTOs for short. Each officer has two of them, a primary and a secondary, for different phases of the FTO process. We were given bullets for our guns and told to load them, an interesting and sober moment for new boots to now have a "hot" weapon in their holster. The rest of week was spent orientating to our new surroundings, reading policy, going over defensive tactics. We were issued our lockers, keys, and other additional equipment. They took us to court one day to watch the proceedings; we toured the high school and met various officials in different departments in town. This week is mainly getting you orientated, and it's not until the following week that you actually begin your FTO period.

Strangely enough, I can't really remember my first ever call, but I remember it was something that was nonsense and uneventful. My first phase of FTO began on the day shift, which is a nice, easy introduction to police work. My primary FTO was a very animated individual who made me laugh most of the time whether he intended to or not.

When you start FTO, you don't do anything by yourself, and you basically just sit there and observe your FTO from the passenger seat. Eventually they have you start by using the radio and getting used to the different police ten codes and terminology. I was pretty natural at this coming from the military; others, however, sounded pretty bad initially, as you could hear their unsureness on the radio. Of course everyone makes mistakes on FTO, and I myself made several.

FTO is a very nerve-racking time; you are constantly being looked at and observed by your FTO from the other seat, as well as by the senior other officers on calls. Once you start driving is when most people really start to fall apart. It's funny how when you have radio chatter, a laptop, and an FTO talking to you how your basic driving skills suddenly fade. It's often common for recruits to make several traffic violations while they aimlessly drive around roads they don't know, trying to multitask and listen to their FTOs. Most of the time, I was yelled at for driving too slow, or blowing a stop sign here or there. Of course this only gets worse when you actually have to go to a call, adding the extra stress in. Now you have to worry about everything being said on the radio and finding the house, all while your FTO is watching you. Afraid to screw up while being observed, you will naturally screw up even more. Emergency calls for service obviously require a faster code response. Code three in my department is lights and sirens for an in-progress call such as a disturbance, serious motor vehicle accident with injuries, medical emergencies, etc.

Imagine yourself driving down a major road somewhere in a cruiser. With your bright strobe lights flashing and siren blaring, you are essentially speeding and very quickly approaching the traffic in front of you. Some cars are moving out of your way, others are not. Cars in front of you are making turns, oblivious to your presence behind them. Cars suddenly pull out or cross traffic in front of you. Your focus at this point is not crashing. At the same time, you are trying to figure out where the heck you are going without looking too lost or flustered in front of your FTO. The radio is abuzz with information from dispatch as well as other officers' radio transmissions. The dispatcher puts a suspect vehicle description and plate that just pulled away from the scene. You don't hear it, however, because you are having auditory exclusion and tunnel vision, driving down the road with your heart racing. Your FTO asks you, "Did you hear that?" Barreling down the road in panic mode, you say no, and he tells you that you just missed an important piece of information and makes a note of it for your evaluation.

This is scenario is common among new recruits and fades away with experience. Twelve years later, I could be going code to a call, eating a sandwich, answering the radio, and talking to my wife on my cell phone at the same time. My wife says, "Is that your siren?" and gets mad at me and orders me to call her back later. It's a natural progression, and multitasking just becomes one of those things you learn to do.

* * * * *

As I mentioned before, I had no shortage of screwups while on FTO. One night I hit a large snow/ice bank with the front of the cruiser while trying to park. Another time I was going code and approaching a hill. My FTO kept on warning me, "Hill! Hill!" But we soon went sailing over the hill, all four tires in the air à la *Dukes of Hazzard*. One time, he actually told me to pull over, then kicked me out of driver's seat on the way to a call.

One of my favorite moments, however, was spilling a fresh iced coffee over one of my FTOs. We had just gone through the drive thru and put our coffees in the cup holders. I then put the arm rest down, which sits above the cup holders, and leaned on it to adjust myself in the seat. The arm rest crushed both iced coffees in a massive explosion that covered the inside of the car. That car forever had the sweet smell of French Vanilla extra, extra iced coffee on the inside of it.

You quickly learn on FTO that you have no clue what you're doing and the academy did not prepare you for anything. Being a cop is not something that just happens when you graduate the academy—you have to experience it. One of my FTOs once told me to expect to have no clue what I was doing at least until my fifth year on the job

It's amazing on FTO how even people on calls for service can even tell you are new. I remember being on a call one night, standing next to my FTO, when the suspect said, "Look at all that shiny new leather and brass. You must new." It's true, recruits just have that new green look, which doesn't just extend to their uniform but their demeanor as well. You can see their innocence as they have not yet developed that callused exterior from years of frustration and discontent with the public. Cynicism and distrust are a natural progression for officers. This comes from years of being lied to and getting irritated with people on calls. If there is one thing you learn quickly on calls is that most people are lying to you to some degree.

There's the saying that there are three sides to every story: yours, mine, and the truth. And this is very true in law enforcement. When talking to people on calls, you begin to get very good at shooting holes in stories and finding contradictions to things that were only said by someone only a few moments ago. People who lie often have a hard time keeping up with their own narratives. It can actually be somewhat amusing to keep catching them and calling them out on a lie. I used to take the position that the first word out of someone's mouth was usually a lie. This skill, however, is one that has to be developed, and as a new boot you often tend to take everyone's word for it.

For instance, you would go serve a warrant, and the wanted person's family member would open the door and tell you they weren't there. You would say, "OK, thanks," then your FTO would push you aside and start grilling the person, eventually getting them to break under pressure. Of course this isn't always the case. Some people might continually lie, but some may also break under pressure when you push them. When you are a new cop, you cannot fathom that someone would lie to a uniformed police officer, and there is an assumption that everyone has a respect for your authority.

One of the most disheartening things I have found is when you are even lied to by someone who would normally be an upstanding citizen. It's so disappointing to have a soccer mom be caught in lie with you—most of the time over something so trivial. Unknown to most people, lying to the police is actually a crime in most places, but it isn't as enforced nearly as much as it could be, or we would be arresting everyone.

People will even go as far as to file false reports to us for their own benefit. This is also a crime, and I have previously charged people with it once I determined them to be lying. It's amazing that people would make up stories and waste our time to commit insurance fraud, cover their own tracks, or to even deceive loved ones.

I once had a husband and wife come in to file a report of fraudulent charges to their bank account. They alleged that someone had accessed their account on an ATM machine and had repeatedly made withdrawals over a period of time. They both stated they never go to that store and do not use that specific ATM for banking. They were very polite and friendly with me at the station and filed all the paperwork, and when I inquired with them if either of them had lost or misplaced their bank card, they said no. This struck me as odd because someone would have needed a bank card to access their account on the ATM. However, there have been cases I have had where criminal enterprises made fake debit cards with stolen card numbers, and I had no reason to distrust this couple.

When I got to work with my investigation and requested video surveillance from the bank, what I got back surprised me. On all the occasions of the transactions, the wife was seen making the withdrawals. I suspected something was up, but giving her the benefit of the doubt, I tried contacting the house several times and left messages for them to contact me in regards to the video surveillance.

Well, she must have not thought I would actually get that far or pull video and did not return any of my phone calls. I even called her husband's cell phone. Shortly after that, she called me and said rather sternly to stop calling her husband and she no longer wanted to pursue the case.

"That's fine," I told her, "but I need you to sign a withdrawal of complaint form."

"I'm not signing anything!" she said. Then she hung up on me. This was a very different person than the nice lady who was joking and laughing with me and her husband at the station.

I responded to the house with the withdrawal form in hand and rang the doorbell.

She came to the door and yelled at me to just leave them alone and stop calling them.

"Look, I don't know what's going on," I said. "You came to me asking for help, and as of right now I have plenty to look into charges for a false police report, so either sign the withdrawal form or that's the route I will go."

She ripped the paper out of my hands and signed it, then slammed the door.

I suspect she was taking money out of the account and must have told her husband that someone was doing it fraudulently to cover herself. I should have charged her, but I wanted to be done with the case.

Car accident and damage reports are also often fabricated. People will claim a ghost vehicle struck their car, but the damage mysteriously doesn't match damage from that of another vehicle.

On one occasion, I responded to speak to a female who claimed she was struck by another vehicle while pulling out onto a main road from a stop sign. First of all if this were the case, it would have been her fault anyway. She described the vehicle, which she said left the scene of the accident, as a small bright-blue car. While checking her vehicle for damage and paint transfer, I noted there wasn't any blue paint on her car but instead I found streaks of white.

When I told her about this, her story changed. "Well, it was a blue car with a white hood."

I then started looking closer at her broken head lights and started picking out little orange plastic shards that looked like they were from construction barrels (which, by the way, often have white stripes on them). At this point, I held up the shards to her. "OK, you still want to stick with your story, or do you want to tell me what you really hit?"

Finally, she admitted she struck a whole bunch of construction barrels in the adjacent town while texting on her phone. I ended up charging her with obstruction and filing a false report.

Another time, I responded to a private business for a hit-and-run accident in the parking lot. The owner met me outside and told me one of her customers' cars was hit and that the suspect vehicle took off. I started talking to witnesses in the area to see if anyone saw anything, and an owner of another business in the plaza said, "Yeah, it was her" (the business owner). He then told me, "She pulled in and whacked his car, and her boyfriend then showed up and drove her vehicle away."

I called for a supervisor, as I was now going to question her. I got her to admit to the accident, and the supervisor advised me to have her bring me to where the vehicle was to finish the report and that we wouldn't charge her this time. After I put her in my cruiser, she told me her boyfriend hid the car in a big box store parking lot. I arrived at the parking lot and literally drove up and down the rows with her until I got to the second to last row. That's when she said, "Yeah, I lied. It's not here, it's at my boyfriend's house."

I was so pissed. I pulled over, yelled, "Get out!," then handcuffed her right there. She had her chance to tell the truth.

* * * * *

People become really weird around the police; their fear and panic sets in and they often do things they would never do. This is why you get the grandma or the school teacher trying to ditch you down a side street when you are going to pull them over. I have found many of working-class people and, yes, even grandmothers hiding in a stranger's driveway waiting for you to pass by. It's always fun to catch these people, but their reactions often vary from apologetic and embarrassed to defensive and angry. "What are you doing, sir?" I would ask. "Do you live here, sir?" They'd usually answer no, looking annoyed, but they already knew I was aware of that, and they'd get so mad that you were calling them out on it.

Another thing you come to realize on FTO is that a lot of people you deal with are often under the influence of something, whether it be drugs or alcohol. I found this especially true when I went to second shift. Come four o'clock in the afternoon, the calls suddenly changed for the worse, as if everyone had been sleeping all day and by then were all liquored up and combative. During second shift, it always seemed to me that everyone on the scene was drunk, even the people that called the police. This makes it especially difficult on calls when trying to decipher who is telling the truth, as everyone in the room is usually intoxicated and lying. It becomes a game of trying to figure out which drunken individual is lying the least.

When you move on further in your FTO training, eventually the FTO steps back and you become the lead officer on calls, trying to talk to people and question them yourself. You haven't learned what questions you should ask and you often you find yourself at a loss for words as the people you are talking to spin drunken lies around you. It's tempting to look at your FTO for help, but at some point you have to display that you are mostly self-sufficient in these scenarios. It's a lot to ask of new police officers who have really only started doing the job weeks ago, but these are skills that become second nature. Becoming seasoned is a matter of progression over the course of your career. Eventually you deal with the same type of calls enough that your skills of discernment become sharpened and you unofficially earn the title "veteran."

CHAPTER 5

A CONFLICT OF INTERESTS: THE CHRISTIAN COP

•

"For the one in authority is God's servant for your good. But if you are do wrong, be afraid, for rulers do not bear the sword for no reason."

ROMANS 13:4 NIV

"**D**o you like being a cop?" my clinician asks me.

As I sit there, I can't help but say, "I don't know, I honestly have always felt to truly love this job you have to be a jerk."

It's not that I hated the job. I guess it would all depend on when you asked me that in my career. It's also important to note that satisfaction (not happiness) in my opinion has a lot to do with the environmental factors, such as what shift you are on, your current supervisors, and the other officers on your shift. These factors can make coming into work bearable or a total nightmare. Every police department has a culture, and each shift usually has its own subculture. I can tell you, a supervisor can ruin everything depending on their personal goals and motives. Make no mistake, everyone is human, and supervisors will play favorites and use their authority to target others. I've seen it happen; it has happened to me. They say that police officers are Type A personalities. To be honest, I'm not really sure exactly what that means, but I don't think it means me.

My friend who is a police officer at another department said to me, "You know, everyone we work with thinks they are an alpha male. Yeah, I'm pretty sure that's not me." He continued, "This job is all that defines them. They're actually losers, really. Without this title, they are nothing, and we are both so much more than that." He then made another valid point: "You know, we're really just wearing a costume. If someone wants to punch us in the face, they're going to do it either way."

I'm pretty sure I'm not an alpha male, but a lot of people I worked with that buy into that mentality. If you think high school was bad, guess again. Imagine a job of predominantly males who are all in competition with each other, constantly trying to portray a specific imagine to their co-workers and please their supervisors. All I can say is, it must be exhausting for those people. I could never do it, and that's why I will always be on the "B team." What is the B team? Well, it consists of everyone with ten or more years who is stuck on day shift patrol and has never made the secret illuminati we call the detectives, or been promoted. At the time I went on leave, my shift consisted of good overlooked officers— officers that aren't overly aggressive with traffic enforcement or with people but rather possess great skills that in our work culture mean nothing. The ability to talk to people with sincerity, empathy, and compassion is a trait I see in some of my other forgotten officers.

We extend love, peace, joy, gentleness, and self-control (see Galatians 5:22–23).

Nobody will ever recognize these traits because that is not what police culture looks for. Supervisors seem to care about one thing—numbers. Your performance as a police officer is determined by your number of arrests and citations, as well as your perception to others. I learned that a co-worker had a citizen call the station to praise their actions on a sudden death call. The caller spoke to a supervisor who answered the phone and was very thankful for the compassion and sympathy showed by the officer when their loved once had passed. The officer had previously told me that the supervisor who took the phone call had always seemed very critical of them. In my opinion as well, this officer displayed what many perceived as arrogance, and from my experience, he generally looked down upon other co-workers that didn't meet his "standards." I am told that after the supervisor got off the phone, he proceeded to tell the officer that the caller was thankful, but then suddenly turned critical, saying, "You think that's what being a good police officer is all about? Well, it's not. You have a job to do. We arrest people, worry about that."

I've always been under the impression being a cop meant being well-rounded, but I guess it's only about arresting people. This is what will ultimately get you somewhere, but who you are depends on a lot on which clique you fall in and who you play golf and drink with.

A co-worker of mine worked like crazy one year, stopping every car under the sun, yielding one of the highest number of traffic stops and arrests in the department. He volunteered for extra duties, which resulted in being called out during all hours of the night, and worked a ton of overtime, stretching himself thin. Whenever a promotion came up, however, he was ultimately skipped over. I've come to recognize that no matter what this guy does, he may never please them.

* * * * *

*Am I now trying to win the approval of human beings,
or of God? Or am I trying to please people? If I were
still trying to please people, I would not be a servant
of Christ.*

GALATIANS 1:10 NIV

I don't like arresting people or giving out tickets anymore. Honestly, I never did. Arresting people does not always help them, yet we are so quick to do it. Giving tickets and towing people's vehicles is supposed to serve as a form of punishment and a deterrent, I guess, but what I have found is that it instead puts people into an endless cycle they cannot get out of. Don't get me wrong, some people are just plain evil and merciless, and they deserve everything they have coming to them by way of the law, but someone once told me something that I'll never forget: "We encounter two types of people: bad people … and good people that just made bad decisions." Although, I can't remember who said this to me, I've always tried to remember that, and I would have to say that the latter of those two types of people are the majority of the people we deal with. Now, that does not mean that people shouldn't be accountable for their actions, but many times, I wonder if arresting the person is helping the situation they or their family are in.

The same principal holds true for traffic violations. The scenario goes like this: Subject A has outstanding traffic fine, which he is trying to pay but can't afford, so his license or vehicle registration gets suspended. Whether or not Subject A realizes this they continue to drive because they need a car to get around and go to work. Subject A will eventually get stopped by an officer, and most likely given some form of physical or citation arrest depending on the laws of the state. The officer will tow his vehicle, which will go to an impound lot, and they will be charged a hefty tow bill and daily impound fees, setting them into further debt and deeper down the rabbit hole. On some of my encounters in this situation, I have found that while the person may not have been the most upstanding citizen in society, they are often trying to get their life back on track and right their wrongs, but the system keeps putting them further into a cycle of no recovery.

Let's now look Subject B. Subject B is a single mother whose vehicle has not passed the state inspection. Her vehicle, while not in brand-new condition, is perfectly operable and it is all she has. She has been told that her vehicle did not pass inspection due to the state emission standards and she would need to replace her catalytic converter, a cost of over two thousand dollars. This repair cost is much more than the value of her fifteen-year-old car. Subject B has an elementary-school-aged daughter who she just finished dropping off at school and is now heading to work to make ends meet. When she had her vehicle inspected, a failure report was sent to the department of motor vehicles and her registration was eventually suspended after a period of specific days. Subject B told me she had X amount of days per the state to rectify the situation, but she just doesn't have money right now, and if she had the money, she would rather use it to buy another used vehicle, instead of dumping money into an vehicle with no value.

In these circumstances I have found that discretion can play a huge role, and sometimes cutting a break to this person has helped me deal with the guilt associated with the nature of this job. As a senior officer in the department, my actions on the street were usually not questioned anymore, as the last supervisor I had was laid-back and not overly critical of our actions. Nevertheless, I was never a producer of numbers, and the longer I was on the job, the more I had an issue with towing vehicles and depriving people of their transportation, which is part of their livelihood. Many newer officers, on the other hand, do not have as much privilege with discretion, but even the ones that do usually never exercise it in the constant chase for higher numbers and boosting their image. Sadly, I've been witness to these newer officers doing things such as towing a person's vehicle after stopping them only a few houses down from theirs. I've even seen young officers tow a vehicle on a holiday and issue tickets on Christmas Day.

Though not very often, I once made this mistake in my younger years and fell into the pressure at times of chasing the numbers, to get the supers off my back. I once stopped a woman with a registration violation, towed her vehicle, then issued her citations when her house was not that far away within town. At the time, I did not have much for the way of numbers for that month and needed to something to show for. Later that night, when I learned this woman was battling the later stages of cancer, I felt absolutely terrible about what I had done and ended up voiding all the tickets. Guess God made a fool out of me that day.

Discretion is not just something we can exercise with traffic but even with arrests. People do not have to be arrested in every situation, and sometimes it's just not the right call to do so. I was once part of search warrant on house suspected of growing marijuana. After we entered the residence, I learned the homeowner, a young woman, had cancer. Her son had started growing marijuana for her medical use; however, she did not have a medical marijuana license by the state. Being the one of the junior officers there, I was told to take her into custody and transport her to the station for booking. Handcuffing this poor woman with her head balding from chemotherapy treatments, I could not help but feel this was morally wrong. Had she committed a crime? Sure, she was growing marijuana without a license. But seriously, once this case got to court, what were they really going to do to her?

As a police officer, I have often been at odds with my job and my own personal moral compass. I once went on a domestic call involving a male, Subject C, we will call him, and his wife. Subject C, a bank manager, had drunk much more than he was used to the night of a big football game. After being dropped off in the early morning hours, his pregnant wife was naturally concerned, as she had not heard from him. Highly intoxicated, Subject C became verbally angry with his wife's questioning and went upstairs, kicking the baby gate at the top, breaking it in the process. Subject C's wife tells us that she got scared, as she has never seen him that intoxicated, and called 911.

When we arrived on scene, Subject C was already in bed asleep in his drunken stupor. The road supervisor on scene observed the broken baby gate on the floor and after listening to the wife's story determined Subject C should be arrested. Subject C's wife was hysterical with this declaration, as she was due with her baby any day and a domestic arrest would leave her alone with the birth of their first child. Subject C, a good person who made a bad decision, was now facing the possibility of spending the weekend in jail, with the chance of his wife going into labor and delivering his firstborn child without him. Subject C would also most likely miss the first month or two of his child's life due to the conditions from a restraining order, automatically put in place by the state. Subject C's wife says that she never intended to have her husband arrested when she called the police. She pleaded with us and insisted that he was a good man and would never hurt her and she was just scared.

Such dilemmas often present themselves on calls, and with your discretion, as limited as it is with domestic situations, comes liability. If you make the decision not to arrest, you better make sure that it does not come back to haunt you and that both parties have been separated for the night. Subject C is a perfect example of how alcohol can do horrible things to good people and come between many relationships.

Wine produces mockers; alcohol leads to brawls.
Those led astray by drink cannot be wise.
PROVERBS 20:1

There is a fine line as a police officer with doing what you feel is right and what is required. This is even harder as Christian, and there will no doubt be times when you feel at odds with your duties. If you are any kind of human being, then some of the things you will do as a cop will place a heavy burden on you, accompanied with guilt. I've been involved with removing children from their homes into state custody and have oftentimes had to arrest parents in front of their small children. This always killed me inside. I absolutely hated it and would be so angry for having to be put into that position. Imagine, a child crying while their parent is being handcuffed and taken away. When I could, I would try to avoid doing this in front of the kids, but sometimes we did not have that luxury. A couple of times, I actually lied to the kids and told them very nicely, Mommy or Daddy had to come with us just to help us with something.

While I always felt these incidents placed an emotional toll on me, it wasn't until recently that I learned that this is actually a separate kind of PTSD called a "moral injury." Although moral injuries can be from guilt resulting from trauma, in some cases, such as the ones I mentioned above, it can also occur from an internal conflict within an officer who may have to enforce a law or make an arrest in something that personally goes against their own moral compass.[1] I can't begin to tell you how difficult these dilemmas can be. Sometime you just have no control over the circumstances, or someone else higher than you makes the decision. But either way the thought, for example, that you may have separated a family, caused more financial hardship, or further traumatized children can be a heavy price on your conscience.

I once heard the argument that being a Christian and a police officer are two things that contradict one another. A Christian exercises forgiveness and principles of turning the other cheek, as taught by Jesus in the Gospels. I am not sure that the two are completely compatible all the time, but from experience I find it is possible yet very difficult. Temptation and darkness are abundant with this job as with any job with authority and power over other people. I believe at the end of the day, there will be circumstances where you either have to please God or please people, and you can't always do both.

---

1. Konstantinos Papazoglou, Ph.D., George Bonanno, Ph.D., Daniel Blumberg, Ph.D., and Tracie Keese, Ph.D., "Moral Injury in Police Work," *FBI Law Enforcement Bulletin*, September 10, 2019, https://leb.fbi.gov/articles/featured-articles/moral-injury-in-police-work.

CHAPTER 6

POMERANIANS, PURSUITS, <u>AND</u> CLOSE CALLS

Show me, LORD, my life's end and the number of my days; let me know how fleeting my life is.
PSALM 39:4 NIV

In a lot of circumstances you come across as a cop, things could go really bad, but there also some instances where the chances are much higher. Vehicle chases, for one, are really dangerous for both the officers and the suspect, not to mention the rest of the motoring public. I've been involved in a few vehicle pursuits, and they can be very nerve-racking. Someone who is willing to run or flee from the police can have the potential for other dangerous and violent actions.

One time, we were chasing an angry individual who was texting his ex-wife with all kind of threats as he drove to her house. We caught up with him and followed him all the way to his ex-wife's house, where he pulled into the drive at full speed, ramming the back of her parked car in the driveway. As the second car in pursuit of him, I saw him smash into her car, making a huge mess of debris and glass. The inertia of the impact made his car roll backward into the street.

I got out of my car and ran toward the vehicle while another officer ran up and started pounding the windows with his baton.

I could see his baton literally bouncing off the glass with no effect.

One thing I learned over the years is that it is really, really hard to break a car window, especially with a baton. You really need a specialized glass breaking tool. I can recall a few other circumstances when I had a sore hand the next day after trying to smash a car window with my baton. One of those instances was during another car chase, and the other was of an individual in a diabetic shock that crashed car into a tree and was still trying to drive away with his foot on the accelerator and the car engine revving. In both instances, I pounded and pounded with my baton while onlookers watched as my baton just kept bouncing off the window. It wasn't until someone showed up with a rescue tool/glass punch that the window would break. After that last incident with the diabetic driver, I broke down and ordered the stupid little eight-dollar tool online.

Driving code in general is dangerous and a very nerve-racking experience where anything can happen. Anytime you are driving at a high rate of speed through traffic you run the risk of being in an accident. It's a known fact that with higher speeds come reduced stopping distance and reaction times. I have had my fair share of close calls going code. I've had oblivious people pull out in front of me and had to swerve out of the way or into incoming traffic. I've also miraculously avoided collision with different wildlife, including deer and coyote that either decided to run or stop in the middle of the street.

On one particular summer day, I actually completely lost control of my cruiser and was spinning around in the middle of the street. It had just lightly rained when the sun came out and it suddenly became really hot. I think that the oils on the surface of the road where lifted and slick from the rain, plus my cruiser tires were relatively bald and the administration was particularly cheap about replacing tires until the winter.

I was heading to a vehicle that had just crashed into a tree with unknown injuries. Driving lights and sirens down the street, I went around a bend and drove over a bump from the sewer cap in the road that was slightly raised. I felt the rear end of my cruiser break loose, and I began to viciously spin 360 degrees down the road. As I was spinning, time almost slowed down and I could see oncoming traffic parting like the Red Sea with vehicles jumping up onto the sidewalk to get out of my way. The vehicle stopped spinning but was now rapidly sliding with my driver's side straight toward a telephone pole and a flower shop. It seemed as though impact was imminent, and then suddenly at the last second, I felt my vehicle tires grip and the car went diagonally to the opposite side of the road and I ended up on the sidewalk. I got out of the vehicle, and there wasn't a scratch on the car or me for that matter. I caught my breath and told dispatch I had just lost control of the vehicle, but it appeared undamaged and that I was continuing on to the call.

Dispatch was already aware of what just happened, though, because a couple people driving by had just called the station, including one frantic lady who was crying hysterically on the phone because she drove by and thought I had crashed.

* * * * *

Along with vehicle chases and code responses, foot pursuits are another scenario where things could go terribly wrong. Foot pursuits can put you in a vulnerable position, especially if you are by yourself. You will get easily winded, and it is common to get disoriented with your location as you cross yards, streets, and wooded areas. If you are by yourself, this could be a big problem, because if you get hurt or the person you are chasing decides to fight you, no one else might know where you are. I've been in a few foot pursuits, but there are two that stick out the most. Both times, however, I was alone during the pursuit.

The first one was more comical than anything. The animal control officer had seen an individual walking who we knew to have outstanding warrants. This individual was a frequent flier with us and had several previous DUI (Driving While Under the Influence) charges with us. He was addicted to pain medication and had smashed into a few cars here and there while driving. He took off in his vehicle one time, and an officer had to pursue him. Another time he ended up crashing up onto a median, and when I pulled up, he was revving his engine, trying to get away, but his vehicle was stuck.

I had been sitting at the skate park, eating my lunch, when the animal control officer pulled up to me and told me he was walking down the road. It was the middle of summer, and it was easily over ninety degrees that day. I found the guy walking shirtless with his little Pomeranian dog while holding an iced coffee. As I pulled alongside him, he picked up the dog and tucked him under his armpit. I exited my car and said, "Hey, John, come here, we need to talk." He threw his iced coffee at me (and missed) and sprinted away, leaping over a picket fence, dog in arms. He had a pretty good lead on me when he went down a bike path then up a berm that led onto a golf course. As I was running after him, I recalled a recent foot pursuit by another officer in which he was heavily criticized by the majority of the department for sounding like a screaming child on the radio because no one could understand him. Being very cognizant of this, I tried to sound as clear as possible over the radio in between heavily sucking in the humid August air.

I can only imagine what it looked like to the people playing golf when a shirtless dude holding a Pomeranian football ran by them, followed by an out-of-breath cop shouting, "COME ON, JUST STOP!" I figured I could appeal to his reason, as we were both most likely extremely tired, but to no avail. As I am chasing him across the golf course, the dispatcher asked for a location update. So I look for the nearest hole and say, "Just north of hole number nine." We went off of the golf course into the woods, across a small stream, through a briar patch, and ended up onto another street, where he was tackled by another officer who pulled up in his cruiser.

Let me just say this: I hate chasing people on foot—I am not a runner, never was. I am by no means fat, but even in the military I was never much of a runner. When I have to run after people, my first thought is to try to catch the person no matter what so I don't get my chops busted later for losing them. Of course over the years, I only caught one person by myself; the rest of the time, there were others there to assist or catch them.

I remember one time we went after a breaking and entering suspect. We didn't have much of a physical description and were checking the area in between all the businesses when he walked out from between two buildings and right where I was standing. I didn't know exactly what he was supposed to look like, but judging by his face upon seeing me and then running across traffic on the main road, I knew he was the guy. I ran after him across the street, praying I would not get struck by a passing car and trying to let everyone know I found him and was in pursuit. As we ran along the opposite side of the road, I was determined to finally catch one bad guy in a foot chase, so I yelled out, "STOP OR I'LL SHOOT!" in an attempt to scare him to stop. To my surprise, he hesitated for a split second but continued to run alongside the main road. Of course, I knew I could not shoot him, but I thought maybe that would get him to reconsider. Then of course, I immediately think, Oh crap, I hope no one else heard that or caught that on camera.

As I start making my way closer to him, I pull out my TASER weapon and figure it's worth a shot at this point. I fire but miss, and because I'm still running, I get caught up in the TASER weapon wires. In case you are not aware how a TASER weapon works, they fire out two probes, which are attached to a thin set of wires. TASER weapon probes stick into the suspect and deliver an electrical pulse into the suspect. Now tangled in my TASER weapon wires, I continue to chase the guy toward an intersection, where a passing motorist tries to intervene by blocking the suspect with his vehicle. The suspect jumps and slides over the hood of the car, crossing the main road again, this time running into the arms of officers from the adjacent towns.

I ended up transporting the suspect back at the station, and he starts talking in the backseat of the car. "Dude, some cop yelled he was going to shoot me," he tells me. "That almost made me stop right then and there. That's crazy, yo."

Yes, shoot you with the TASER weapon, that is. At least that's my story, and I'm sticking to it.

* * * * *

When I was still relatively new on the job, I was patrolling the more rural end of town one day and was sitting in a parking lot typing a report. I got a call for a suicidal male with a gun, and the address just happened to be exactly diagonal across the roadway where I was parked. Our western end of town is relatively isolated, and backup can be realistically twelve to fifteen minutes away. I pulled across the street, beyond the house to park out of view of it, but it was already too late—the suspect and the caller (his wife) had seen me already across the street.

As I am trying to stay at a distance behind the bushes by the curb, the wife starts calling out to me, "HELP, PLEASE! HE HAS GUN, HE IS GOING TO HURT HIMSELF. DO SOMETHING."

A second later, her husband comes to the door and says, "OFFICER, LISTEN, I'M NOT GONNA DO ANYTHING," and throws a rifle onto the front lawn. He then starts to walk outside of the house, where his wife is and, more importantly, the rifle. Now, I was later reprimanded for what I did next, because apparently I was supposed to just remain where I was and "set up a perimeter."

As the guy walks outside, I decide that I need to now take control of the situation, as I don't want him near the gun on the lawn. I move forward with my gun drawn, then order him to the ground and not to move.

Immediately the wife and her daughter run up to me and start screaming at me, "DON'T SHOOT HIM! PLEASE."

"I'm not going to shoot him," I said while they are screaming over my shoulder.

I run up between the car and the suspect and grab the rifle on the lawn that's only a few feet from him and throw it behind me near the car. Meanwhile, I can hear from on the radio, backup is still a ways away. I begin to think, I can't just sit here for fifteen minutes with this guy like this and his family screaming at me, so I decide to handcuff him.

"I'm going to handcuff you," I said. "Just lay flat, keep your hands behind your back, and don't move,"

"OK, Officer, whatever you say. This is all just a big misunderstanding."

I move up and handcuff him without any problems and sit him on the steps. The radio is still ablaze with craziness of people trying to respond to the scene, and I can't really get a word in. Finally, I said, "CLEAR THE AIR, HE'S BEEN SECURED."

A higher-up shows up on scene and starts telling me I should have set up a perimeter and waited for backup. "What were you thinking?" he says rather angrily.

To be fair, this guy was not a tactics guy, but being new I didn't have much say. I made sure to stick up for myself, though. I said, "Sir, he came out of the house, and he was in between me and the gun, and I wasn't going to let him get close to that gun, kill her, kill me, or himself." I continued, "With respect, sir, you were not there. I took control of the situation. I come from the military, where sometimes action is better than inaction. That's the difference between living and dying."

"Well," he says, "you might end up getting disciplined for this."

"OK, that's fine," I said. "No one got hurt, and I did what I felt was necessary."

As word got out around the department, I began to garner a lot of support from other supervisors and most patrolmen. A lot of guys applauded my actions based on the circumstances. One supervisor in particular said, "What the hell did they want you to do when the guy came out of the house? Say, 'SIR, SORRY BUT MY BACK UP ISN'T HERE YET. CAN YOU PLEASE GO BACK INSIDE'?"

To this day, I stand behind my actions. There is nothing I felt I should have done differently. Sometimes things just unfold a certain way and you have to go with it. The guy came out of the house, and I made sure I did not let him control the situation. I never did get any disciplinary action from it either. They weren't expecting me to defend myself like I did either. I may have been new, but I wasn't a child. You pay us to carry a gun for crying out loud; don't second-guess everything we do and treat us like children.

While I could go on and on about some of the crazy calls I have been on, just know that there were plenty more, but these are some of the more memorable moments. When all this is said and done, I intend to find out my total number of calls I have been on since my first day of the job. Our computer system is able to categorize and look at the different types of calls for service we have responded to and maybe I will pull the tallies in by the end of this book. Again, this book may eventually serve as guidance in some form or another to others, but it is also a way for me to document my career in this whole process.

CHAPTER 7

FLESH, FORGIVENESS, AND THE COST OF HUMAN NATURE IN POLICING

For the flesh desires what is contrary to the Spirit, and the Spirit what is contrary to the flesh. They are in conflict with each other.

GALATIANS 5:17 NIV

Our flesh is the human side of our nature, which is full of sin. Our flesh makes us jealous, mean, prejudiced, and vindictive, among other things. These human qualities don't dissipate when someone puts on a uniform of authority, but in some cases they are amplified and hidden behind a badge. This is apparent in the way police officers treat each other and especially citizens on the street.

As a new police officer, one of the main things that discouraged me in the very beginning was that some the senior officers would talk to people on calls. Some officers could be very demeaning, indirectly poking fun and mocking people while speaking with them. I came to learn rather quickly that this behavior often carried onto their co-workers, as they would often criticize other cops and cutting down various people within the department.

We are all sinners; I don't want to throw stones, because we are human and each of us has our own issues we have to deal with. I had my own sins that I had to face during all of this. Sins that I was guilty of. Sins that I needed to get past to move on in my journey of faith. I can only pray for these individuals too at this point so that they change the way that his presence is being reflected to others, because he has the ability to be better.

"Outwardly you look righteous, but inwardly your hearts are filled with hypocrisy and lawlessness" (Matthew 23:28).

Here Jesus is speaking directly to the "teachers of religious law." Jesus accuses them of worrying about cleaning "the outside of the cup and the dish" yet inside they are "filthy-full of greed and self-indulgence." Reading this, I feel like I am being shown not to be deceived by those who carry themselves one way on the outside, yet their actions show what's really inside them. I always got the impression that some officers viewed people, especially criminals, as if they are inferior beings and policing was the way to bring the sword of justice among them. I can't help but feel that this is wrong. While I have seen many examples of Scripture condemning the wicked and those who murder and commit crimes, I am by no means without sin myself, and I try not to treat the people we deal with on calls like dogs.

An interesting scripture I recently read brought this to light. I could not help but initially feel confused about how Jesus was portrayed dealing with a Canaanite women who came to him begging for help to save her demon-possessed daughter.

In Matthew 22–28, Jesus appears to almost ignore or dismiss the woman while walking with his disciples. He essentially tells her that he is only there for "the lost sheep of Israel." This woman is portrayed as pestering Jesus and the disciples wanted to send her away. Jesus then tells her in parable form that food which belongs to children should not be thrown to the dogs, almost as if he is saying you are not worthy of his miracles. This bothered me initially after reading this, as I thought Jesus was calling her a dog and would only heal God's people. What I find more interesting is the Canaanite women's answer, "Yes, it is Lord; even the dogs eat the crumbs that fall from their master's table." I interpret the "dogs" in my application as criminals or even the people living poor lifestyles. Police officers very frequently deal with both, and both are worthy of God's "crumbs."

Jesus was an interesting teacher; he often used parables and other out-of-the-box methods to illustrate his point to his disciples. Jesus praised this woman in front of the disciples for her faith, and the woman's daughter was instantly healed. I believe Jesus was not purposely ignoring the woman but teaching both her and the disciples at the same time about faith and perhaps testing the woman and his disciples. Jesus appeared to always have a method and a message to all of his actions and words. This is very apparent from the depictions of him in all of the Gospels. Everything he said and did was for the purpose of showing God's power and his glory. Jesus knew he was there to spread the message about the kingdom of heaven, but he also knew that many, including his own followers, would not fully understand, so he chose to use parables to illustrate many of his points in regards to sin and faith. He was also trying to prepare his disciples for ministry so that after he departed they would be able to spread the word as well. Besides the story about the Canaanite woman, we know that Jesus did not only come to save his people but came to save Gentile sinners as well.

I would observe many officers who would belittle or treat

people poorly. A lot of people that police officers come across are plagued by darkness. Depression, suicidal thoughts, and substance addiction are common things we see among our dealings with the public. Not everyone plagued by darkness is a bad person, but some may be living more sinfully than others. I always tried to remember that all of these people are also human and more frequently also God's lost children. In Matthew 11:15, one of the disciples is asked by a Pharisee, "Why does your teacher eat with such scum?" Jesus replied, "Healthy people don't need a doctor. Sick people do." He then tells them to learn the meaning of mercy and says, "For I have come to call not those who think they are righteous, but those who know they are sinners."

I am guilty myself of using the word scum when referring to certain people, and for that I ask for forgiveness. I never, however, would ridicule nor do this to anyone's face, but I have seen plenty of other officers do this. It was not uncommon to see officers argue with, pester, and antagonize someone mouthy who was locked up in the cell block and think, What are you doing? Who cares what they are saying?

Some officers take this job way too personally. I swear some officers just get a charge out of this, but you become no better than the person in handcuffs, if not worse. There have been plenty occasions when after the officer walked away, I would have to whisper to the suspect to just be quiet and ignore the officer if he engaged him. Hey, I was honest, I knew who were the instigators were, and I wanted to keep things civil with the suspect. I often would tell people I arrested, "It's not personal. I'm just doing my job, and this is how I feed my family." Unfortunately that's not how many cops think, and some actually do have vendettas or chips on their shoulder, and that can create bad relationships with the public.

* * * * *

Although I have not personally witnessed much excessive force, I have, however, seen a few actions by officers that have gone too far. One night when I was new, we were chasing a guy who was wielding a large piece of wood during a foot pursuit through the woods. It was dark, wet, and swampy, and I fired my TASER weapon as I got close to the guy but missed. Moments later, another officer's TASER weapon made contact with the guy, and he instantly went down. As I was handcuffing him, another officer suggested to me, "You could give him a couple of shots if you want." Of course, I didn't oblige because that is not only against my own ethics—it's downright wrong.

I've never understood why someone would strike someone who is already subdued and/or handcuffed. We are taught this is excessive force in the academy, so why do officers still think they can do this? Many years ago, way before my time as a cop, there was the mentality that if you ran from the cops and got caught, you were going to catch a beating. Those days are gone, and not only is it not right, but with all the cells phones and recording technology out there, why would you do this? There becomes a fine line when cops take things too personally and you let your flesh take over. I realize your adrenaline surges in these scenarios; heck, I've yelled and sworn at people who ran from me. When I caught them, it's hard not to, but once they are caught, the game is over; I've never been tempted or possessed to strike them after the fact. Just because we are enforcers with given authority does not give us the right to go beyond our duties.

When any kind of power comes, cops are not exempt from this temptation. Unfortunately, when I arrived my first day at the station, I thought cops in today's society were all well-educated professionals now, unlike their brethren from years past. It did not take me long, however, to see how human flesh can translate behind the badge.

There was a memorable moment when I was new when we got a call from a drunk person stumbling in the roadway at night. After I located the person on the side of the road, I did my checks, ran his ID, and was ready to give him a ride home. The individual was not drunk enough to be hospitalized, and I contacted a family member who was home to care for him. Being fresh out of the academy, I was courteous, polite, and professional to him, using the "verbal judo" I was taught in the academy to deescalate the situation and get him to comply. The senior officer I was with, however, took issue with this, and soon as we got the individual in the car, he began to rile him up. He then looks at me as the guy starts to get angry and says, "Oh yeah, I'm going to get this guy to fight you by the time we get to his house." I couldn't believe it, I thought I did well handling the call without anyone getting hurt, and here was this senior officer purposely trying to cause an altercation. I remember back then only weeks on the job being uncomfortable and thinking, Is this how it's going to be?

At one point one particular officer became a supervisor midway in my career, and I felt as though he tried to turn people against me. I was told by other guys he would ridicule me to them when I wasn't around. I always felt he would do whatever he could just to make things difficult for me. The good thing was that other people saw it was happening and stepped in. Later on, some officers had even approached me and apologized that they were guilty of laughing along with him at my expense. During this period, I dreaded coming to work and was literally brought to tears over it several times.

This is an example of how our words and actions can have a severe effect on someone. I'm sure this officer wasn't considering the anguish I was going through over this or just did not care. This should be an example of why we should use our words to pick others up and not put them down. Our mouths are capable of inflicting so much harm. The enemy gets to people and uses their tongues as a weapon to injure others.

> *Let no corrupting talk come out of your mouths, but only such as is good for building up, as fits the occasion, that it may give grace to those who hear.*
> EPHESIANS 4:29 ESV

I use the above scripture to illustrate two points: to address this officer's behavior toward me but also my behavior later in regards to him. As the years passed, I became very distrusting and sour after what he put me through. I held a grudge against him for the longest time. Years later I would still let his words continue to harm me by reliving them. I would become angry and aggravated while thinking about my persecution, as it brought back memories of a hard time. I have come to learn that holding onto these negative feelings attached with anger and resentment is toxic. After that time, I had also become very defensive to the point that if I thought someone said something critical or antagonizing to me about my performance at work, even as a joke, I would get snappy with them.

Cops in general have a bad habit of putting down other officers in front of each other as a way to make themselves look better. What better way to hide your own insecurities and errors than to draw attention to someone else's.

I felt like I was always overly sensitive to this, especially after my time of persecution. I did not want things to go back to the way they were before during that time. I've always felt that certain officers who never even worked with me had an impression of me from some of the negative mentally being spread. When these officers did work with me, many had no issues with me and realized their prejudice was misplaced and also a symptom of trying to fit in.

Eventually what happens to people who continuously target and mock people is that they are exposed for what they really are. This behavior became so visible among one supervisor that the administration would not even let him conduct yearly evaluations of certain officers because they felt they he would not be fair as he openly displayed prejudice against them. Unfortunately what happened to me was not isolated, and there are various other examples of supervisors that held personal vendettas against officers for various reasons.

"For those who exalt themselves will be humbled, and those humble will be exalted."
LUKE 14 : 11

During my very recent struggle at home on leave, I had to bring myself to forgive anyone who "trespassed against me" and continually remind myself not to hold on to it. This is a work in progress, because it can be extremely difficult to love and forgive someone that persecuted us. The Bible is very clear on forgiveness of others and very simply states in several different areas of the Gospels that we must forgive others if we ourselves want to be forgiven. With that said, even writing all this down, I am hoping to move on from it for good. I apologize for any remaining bitterness and judgement in my writing. I am entitled to my opinions, and I was also reflecting upon how certain individuals were described by others. We all have experiences in our lives with persecution from other people. All I can do is remember to pray for those who persecuted me and that they truly become right with God and that this is reflected in their actions toward others as well and not just from their outwardly "perception." Let this story and the following scripture be words for all of us to remember, most of all myself included: "Don't speak evil against each other, dear brothers and sisters. If you criticize and judge each other, then you are criticizing and judging God's law" (James 4:11).

The good news was, eventually I got off my FTO period, and after you complete your probationary year, you can handle calls and traffic for the most part how you want. This is obviously also dependent on your current supervisors and whether they are present on your calls or not. As you get more time on, you get more freedom and discretion and as such you will not want supervisors coming to your calls. The wrong supervisor could create more unnecessary work and problems for you, as their methods may not be in line with yours.

I can't tell you the amount of times I've told people on traffic stops, "Get out of here before my supervisor shows up" because I did not want to be forced to issue a ticket, tow a car, or make an arrest for nonsense. I learned a lot on FTO, but mostly I learned what kind of cop I did not want to be. Unfortunately the kind of cop I chose to be is often the kind that will never make any progress. Unless you are willing to lay the hammer on the motoring public and stab each other in the back, then you will most likely rot on patrol division. One officer once described to me that moving ahead in the department was like being on the television show Survivor in that you had to know how to just play the game. I was never really into selling my soul to be promoted or favored. At the end of the day, I have to sleep at night and be comfortable with who I am and the decisions that I made.

Day shift patrol is where most forgotten officers go to their career death, at least in my department. You become labelled a "day shift guy" by all the other young newbies who have reached that three- to five-year mark, and all of a sudden think they are super cop. They haven't yet reached that point in their career where they have become tainted and tired. They still think there is a chance for them to make detectives or narcotics, and they sell their souls to the right people to make sure they don't look like a "load" and end up like one of those day shift guys. Geez, they don't even carry flashlights on their belts anymore—they aren't real cops!

To some extent it is true that priorities tend to change for officers who have over ten years of service and end up on day shift. There is saying at my department that "day shift is a choice." This means that the people who chose to be on day shift are essentially digging their own grave. The guys on second and third shift dread working day shift because they have been told that it sucks. And you're surrounded by the administration all day, they micromanage you, and God forbid you have to go into the station for something, some administrator might give you a hard time for not being on the road. And those day shift guys, they aren't team players; they forgot how to be real cops.

This, of course, is all nonsense, and it's just a mentality that the young guys have developed. There will be a day when they get married or have kids, and the temptation of a semi-normal work schedule working days is really nice. OK, so as a day shifter, you have to get used to certain things that the other shifts don't have to bother with. For starters, I have found that most administrators don't usually bother you if you have a valid reason to be in the station and you are not just hanging around. The traffic during the day is also kind of a challenge, as you're not just patrolling empty dark streets and parking lots, so it's harder to go after cars and pull people over with more congestion on the roadways. It's also light out and you're more visible to the motoring public, so you have to get used to be stared at by every passing motorist.

The motoring public during the day also generally consists of working-class people, so getting "good grabs" on car stops is a lot harder to find if you're into such things. Day-shift car stops mostly yields minor violations like suspended licenses and other moving vehicle and registration violations. This is boring to most young cops, who want to be snagging drugs and other nefarious things that lurk around during the darker hours.

Day shift patrol also consists of a lot of paperwork and follow up investigation that can be time consuming. Most of the calls for civil complaints, larcenies, and breaking and entering are discovered and called in during the day hours. This often makes me the need to remind people that the police department is open twenty-four hours a day and people don't need to wait until the morning to report everything. So yes, day shift has its negatives: You tend to get all the discoveries from the night before when people wake up, to include a lot of dead bodies from overnight, but it's worth it when you go home when it's still light out and you can have dinner with your family.

When I first got on the job, day shift was sought after; it was the next step before you got to detective. Detectives were mostly selected based on when it was your turn seniority-wise, but with certain people in charge that mentally changed drastically. Our "process"—if you want to call it that—to become a detective has changed several times over the course of the years. The general idea centers around this, though, is that nobody really knows how you become one. There are no tests, no seniority points, no education points—nothing. The process used to be you submit your name, and they just chose "best fit." After the union argued there needed to be a process, they came up with an idea where all the shift lieutenants would meet and supposedly rank you in different categories such as integrity, dedication, work ethic, etc. The problem is, the process is very subjective, and supervisors are ranking you that don't work with you, so they are going to skew the numbers to get their own people in higher rankings.

Some administration and important figures in the department have also been suspected of influencing the supervisors to put certain people at the top of the list, even though they are not supposed to do this. Magically, when a detective process happens, everyone seems to already know who is going to come out in the top three positions and ultimately get the position. This creates a lot of bad blood and a negative atmosphere in the department every time a process is done. As I mentioned earlier, people feel like the same people keep getting promoted and selected, or a lot of it has to do with their associations and "perception" of them, not such much their own qualifications.

Being a new guy introduced into a new culture, and all these things can be intimidating and confusing. When I would meet new guys, I would often tell them to remain humble, to not let the job consume them, and to remember this is only a fraction of their life. I tell them, "Despite what some people will tell you here, it's not all about the job." When I was new, one of the senior officers tried to tell me that the job was more important than my family. This is so far removed from the truth.

I tell new guys, even though eventually they will all drink the Kool-Aid and fall into the trap, "Remember that the day you leave, the department lives on without you. No one leaves a legacy behind. There are no framed jerseys in the hallway with your name on it, no statues erected of you—nobody cares. You are lucky if they grill some hamburgers in the backlot and give you a cheap plaque that says something like 'Thanks for Your Service.' The next day, everyone goes back to work and no one blinks an eye."

I've seen various retirees stop into the station for something, and they often comment that they don't recognize anyone and nobody even waves to them. I'm not sure what they expected. This is the nature of this job: You are a tiny blip on the radar screen. You are washed up and no longer of value when you leave.

I couldn't help but feel the same way myself with what I went through. Once I was out on leave, I barely had any communication from the administration, and no administrators reached out to ask me how I was doing. I had officers text me here and there, and I am extremely grateful of that. This process has left me with so many feelings, and strongest among them is the feeling the department and the town abandoned me and are now writing me off and refusing to accept responsibility and help me.

I hear this treatment is standard of first responders. One of them told me, "Once you're no longer of use to them, they don't care. They don't care you got PTSD from serving the town, and they will do everything in their power to not have to take care of you or pay you out."

Gee, thanks for the support.

CHAPTER 8

ANIMALS, ODDITIES, AND THE ABSURD

"He will once again fill your mouth with laughter and your lips with shouts of joy."
JOB 8:21

I'd be lying if I say this job was all bad and did not have any absurd moments. There is a lot to be said about finding humor in things. I also feel that it will be helpful to think of some of the more humorous moments in my career, so I don't just associate it with the parts that are affecting me.

Ecclesiastes 3:3 speaks about "A time to heal. A time to tear down and a time to build up. A time to cry and a time to laugh." God wants us to laugh; it is no mystery that laughter makes us feel good and releases certain chemicals in the brain. It's why we hear medical professionals and evangelists preach about it. The saying that "laughter is the best medicine" really is biblical. Proverbs 17:22 also says: "A cheerful heart is good medicine, but a broken spirit saps a person's strength."

For police officers, laughter is necessary for your sanity. There are just some times when all you can do is laugh about what you are seeing or hearing. We deal with such craziness in the world that sometimes, it's just plain funny. But we need to be careful because laughter can also be a cover-up. We often hear about "sick humor," which with police officers is very common, whether this is making light of certain grotesque calls or circumstances that we come across. Through my journey with PTSD I've come to see that I have been guilty of this myself as a means of coping, and even Scripture seems to reaffirm this.

"Laughter can conceal a heavy heart, but when the laughter ends, the grief remains" (Proverbs 14:13).

Look, a lot of cops are more bothered by things they see and do than they let on. I myself covered up for years and presented myself as a tough guy, but now when people call to ask me how I am doing, I can almost detect the pain in their voices, as they seem to be quietly reflecting on and relating to what I am saying to them, and my bringing it up is making them uncomfortable. Sure, I can hear their breathing rate change and their sighs of stress when talking to them about my issues. But I know they haven't reached the point I have yet, and they will continue to bury their pain and do their jobs, as it is their livelihood, and for their sake I pray they never do reach that point.

For now, let's focus on the positive, healthy type of laughter.

* * * * *

I'm going to start off with a story that for me initially was not very funny, but to others it was hysterical.

I was responding to a house alarm and in the process of checking the exterior of the residence. The house was a really nice Cape-style house on a huge piece of property. The front lawn was ginormous as well, and as it turned out, there was an invisible dog fence surrounding the entire front yard. As I made my way around the back corner of the house, I spotted two Weimaraners at the other corner of the yard. For those not familiar with these dogs, they are rather large silver hunting dogs. Apparently they can be very aggressive by nature, and I can attest to this. As soon as they saw me, they were on me in a matter of seconds. These things were like a pack of raptors out of a scene of Jurassic Park and were synchronized in their attack. I really didn't even have time to run, and even If I did, I would have never made it beyond the safety of the electric fence.

I started to stumble backward and draw my TASER weapon as one of them was about to bite me. The dog was literally in mid launch toward my groin when I shot him with the TASER weapon. I'm pretty sure I only had a matter of milliseconds, but everything suddenly slowed down as the lead dog launched toward me in mid jump with jaws wide open. I then heard the pop! of the TASER weapon before I even realized I had pulled the trigger.

Now in TASER weapon training, they tell you to hit an animal, it is best to turn the TASER weapon sideways and lengthwise of the animal. Well, let me tell you this dog was so close to my crotch that both TASER weapon probes hit him directly in the mouth. Immediately the dog dropped as stiff as a board while I started to back up as far as I could. The other dog took one look at his friend and ran away into the field in the back of the woods. While the dog is getting juiced, I felt really bad for it but also very relieved I didn't get mauled by two dogs. I called the whole ordeal out over the radio, requesting that animal control respond to the scene. Then I got back in my cruiser, and my cell phone started ringing. I answered, still out of breath, and all I heard on the other end of the phone was hysterical laughing from one of the other officers.

Looking back at this now, it is kind of funny. Oh, and if you are concerned about the dogs, they were perfectly fine. The owner, however, was pissed, at least until the animal control officer told him that he was lucky I did not shoot the dog with my gun instead. Turns out both of these dogs had previous bite histories recorded by the local animal hospital. Going forward, according to an email sent out by the administration, we were not going to physically check the residence anymore due to my incident with the dogs.

Dogs and animals in general always seem to provide some comic relief in police work. I was checking a residence on a house alarm one day with a female co-worker of mine. We had pretty much worked together in the same platoon since day one together and have our fair share of funny stories. While checking the residence we accidentally let the owner's dog out of the house. This dog was so happy to be out of the house that the more we tried to get him back in, the more he thought we were playing with him. We would stop chasing him and kneel down, and he would come close. Then the moment you moved, he would happily wag his tail and dart away, waiting for you to chase him. There was no way we could leave without putting this dog back in the house (I wouldn't want someone to let my dog out).

This went on for about ten minutes with this dog happily taunting us until finally I said to my partner, "Let's go up on the porch and just ignore him." So we pretended he wasn't there and were just sitting on the porch of this house as if we were having a conversation and he didn't exist. And sure enough, when he figured out we were not longer playing his game, he decided to come up on the porch.

At this point my female partner starts cootsie-cooing him. "Come here, sweetie. Who's a good doggy? That's right, you are. Come here." This tactic appears to work, and when the dog gets close enough within reach, she grabs him by the collar and screams, "BAD DOG!" Even I jumped when she did this. Then she proceeds to put him back in the house, looks at me, and makes this psycho half smile and laugh.

* * * * *

Animals always bring some degree of humor to this job. Being from a town with a mixed urban and rural population, it was not uncommon to get calls for horses and cows in the roadway. I made the mistake of trying to pet a horse once and accidently poked it in the eye. My supervisor later yelled at me not to touch animals. I have played crossing guard to many wildlife, to include snapping turtles, turkeys, and—my all-time favorite—a momma duck and her tiny ducklings trying to cross a busy road. It's in moments like these that you see the beauty in nature and all of God's creation.

There are other times with animals, however, that are not so pleasant. When wildlife is injured or sick and we are called, people tend to be under the misconception that we are going to provide medical care. Injured wildlife have to put down (shot); that's pretty much all we can do. I have always hated it because I do not like killing anything. I even try to spare insects that I find in my own house, when I can, by letting them outside. I had gotten into the habit of praying for animals I've had to put down and one time even laid a gloved hand on an injured deer. I know common belief is that animals may not go to heaven or have souls, but we do not know this for sure and they deserve some compassion anyway.

One time, I had gotten a call for an injured and rabid possum in the roadway. When I showed up, the thing was right smack in the middle of a residential street. I didn't think it was safe to shoot it on the pavement, so I tried to get it over to the grass. But this thing was angry—snarling, snapping at me, foaming at the mouth. I took my baton out and tried to give it some love taps to guide it to the side of the grass. The thing was biting and clawing away at my baton, so I start rolling it over and dragging with my baton, which I am sure looked awful by anyone looking.

Finally, a woman comes out of a house and yells at me, "STOP DRAGGING IT! JUST PICK IT UP!"

"Are you crazy? I'm not getting rabies," I said, continuing to drag it across the ground with my baton as it's hissing at me. This was not one of my finest moments, but sometimes there isn't any other way to get the job done.

Another time, an animal control officer (ACO) had called for help putting a rabid groundhog down. Our animal control officers are not authorized to carry guns but are issued OC spray and a baton. When I pulled up in front of the house to assist him, I noticed a large orange OC spray stain on the grass in the front yard, then heard the ACO yelling from the back yard. I found him on his back, cornered by the groundhog, who—now pissed off even more from being sprayed—is snapping, hissing, and closing in on him from only feet away. The ACO yells, "SHOOT HIM! QUICK!"

I take out my gun and quickly fire a few rounds into the grass, missing him and the ACO thankfully. The ACO then grabs his pole and whacks the groundhog, briefly stunning him, as I run up and lay a few rounds into him. This was also not one of my finest moments but one that was funny afterward.

* * * * *

When you work with the same people in your platoon, you tend to always get stuck on the same calls together—for better or for worse. And it's these funny moments you take with you. We were going to another house alarm one day (yes, they are fairly common), and one of the doors was unlocked. Our policy dictates that when we find an unsecured door, we have to make entry and clear the house. We are also required to do so with our service weapon out.

As we entered the house, there is a sign near the door that says "Caution, Beware of Dog" with a picture of a mean-looking German shepherd on it. As soon as we enter the house, the audible alarm starts sounding from our motion in the house. These are extremely loud and ear piercing. We soon pass by a tired-looking basset hound lying on the couch that just as easily dismisses us with a quick glance.

"You must be the attack dog," I say as I walk by.

As we make our way upstairs, the alarm is still blaring away and my female partner sees someone lying in bed. Standing there with her gun out and the alarm blaring, she looks at me and says, "Is she dead?"

"I don't know, how could anyone sleep through this?" I respond.

My partner walks over and pokes at her. "Miss ... miss."

The woman wakes up, sees my partner, and looks at me, then starts screaming hysterically like the lady in the shower scene from Psycho.

"Ma'am, ma'am, police," I said. "It's all right, your alarm is going off."

It took her a few seconds to get her bearing, but she finally laughed and said, "Oh my God, I was passed out. I didn't hear anything."

It's often funny when things are not always what they seem. And it's funny but also kind of sad how we automatically assume everyone is dead on calls.

On another house alarm, I was checking the residence in an elderly trailer park community with another buddy of mine, and we had an unlocked door. We started checking the trailer, and I was following him as he was about to enter the bedroom. But before I could make it through the door behind him, he turned around so quick that plowed right into me.

"OH MY GOD, SHE'S DEAD!" he yelled.

I went into the bedroom, and it appeared like someone was lying under the covers. Together we both winced as we rapidly threw back the covers—only to discover nothing but pillows. I'll never forget my friend's reaction—he literally almost knocked me over, running out of the bedroom, and I couldn't stop laughing about his frantic panic.

Another time, an officer and I were walking around a residence doing a check of the exterior. We tried to get into the backyard, but the yard was surrounded by a chain-link fence, so the officer I was with decided to try to climb over the fence. Determined to take the path of the least resistance, I continued to walk around the fence line and discovered a gate on the side of the yard. As I'm walking into the back yard, I hear the sound of ripping and "AH, WHAT THE [explicit]!" I look up, and the other officer is straddling the middle of the fence with his pants torn wipe open at the crotch, exposing his red heart boxers.

What struck me more than anything was this: There would have been no need to climb the fence at all if he had just walked around the house and found the gate. Standing there in the middle of the yard, I could not stop laughing, looking at him in his shredded pants with his boxers hanging out. What makes it even funnier was how pissed he was. Even as we left the call, I could not stop hysterically laughing to myself.

* * * * *

Sometimes, things aren't funny at the time, but later on when you reflect on them, you find the humor. My buddy and I were once dispatched to a breaking and entering at a local machine shop right at the beginning of the shift. The owner came in and caught the guy trying to break into the register, then started chasing him with a crowbar. It was the middle of winter and a whopping eight degrees outside. As soon as we got there, we confirmed that the owner was holding a crowbar and chasing the suspect. Of course, I did not know who was who at this point and just saw a guy chasing another guy with a crowbar.

My buddy pulled up first on scene and jumped out after the two, followed by me shortly afterward. We then ran after both parties, who went onto a field behind the business. At this point, I am now at a full sprint, following my buddy, who is trying to catch up to the two guys. I hit a patch of ice and almost take a dive, so now I am doing a wobbly high-knee dance as I skate over the patch of ice. We end up on the field behind the building, which is covered with about a foot or so of snow.

Eventually my buddy catches up to both of them and throws the suspect down into the snow and starts wrestling with him. Then I catch up, and we handcuff him facedown in the snow. Suddenly, we both realize how out of breath we are laying there beside the suspect. My lungs are now stinging with sharp pains from sucking in the single-digit air temperature. Neither one of us has enough wind to talk on the radio at this point, because we are both gasping.

Finally, I grab my radio and my buddy looks at me.

"You got this?" he chokes out.

I nod and get out a harsh "thirty ... four ... [my badge

number]. One … in custody" over the radio.

As my buddy walked him out near the front of the business, we notice the suspect's pants had fallen down around his ankles during the chase. This kid had cargo pockets full of all kinds of crap that he had taken from people's cars in the area too.

As we start pulling stuff out of his pockets, he keeps saying, "That's all my stuff."

Then I see a cigar holder with David Jacobs inscribed on it. (I happened to know David Jacobs, a local firefighter who lived in the area.)

"This is your cigar holder?" I ask.

"Yup."

"And you're David Jacobs, right?"

"No," he says, rather cocky.

"OK," I say. "What are you doing with his cigar holder then?"

Dumbfounded, the kid decides to go to his default answer: "It's all my stuff."

Sometimes I don't know if people are just too dimwitted (forgive me, Lord) to know they are caught or think denial will ultimately save them.

After this call, I felt like I blew my lungs out and had this nasty chest cough for about a month afterward. While not funny at the time, it is funny to remember how much discomfort and out of breath the two of us where in that moment that we couldn't even talk, and this was a moment we would often laugh about later. "War stories," as we call them, provide some levity when they are told after the fact. Remembering certain moments and retelling stories, I believe, are good for morale as long as they are healthy and do not fall into too much of the dark humor.

* * * * *

Oftentimes, humorous events can arise out of intense moments and sometimes involve other officers' misfortune. We have seen our fair share of misfortune that turned out to be funny. We had one officer who fell into a covered in-ground swimming pool during a residence check at night. Another officer fell waist deep into a septic tank, and another crashed his cruiser into a lake.

While I never ripped my pants or crashed into a lake, I can recall one incident when I ran into a bee nest while apprehending a suspect. It happened one summer when another officer observed a suspect steal something out of someone's yard. When he went to go stop him, the suspect took off on foot into the neighborhood and the officer lost sight of him. We suspected he was still hiding in the area, so I showed up to help search the area.

While checking one of the yards, we located him behind some garbage cans between two houses. I went to climb over an old wooden picket fence, which was about chest high, to get to the suspect from the adjacent yard. In the moment of trying to cross it, the old weathered fence broke with my straddling it. After crashing to the ground on my side, and quickly jumping up, I ordered the suspect to come out.

Refusing to come out, he kept saying, "I can't move … the bees!"

Of course, at the time I did not see any bees, and I was focused on getting him, so I went into the trash cans and pulled him out and on the ground. As I kept telling him to put his hands behind his back, he kept screaming, "AHH, THE BEES!"

Oblivious to the bees that were actively stinging me, I thought the guy was full of crap and kept yelling at him to shut up and put his hands behind his back. Needless to say, I ended up getting stung around nine times but felt nothing during the moment because of my adrenaline. I also had to notify the neighbor that I broke his fence, but thankfully he was OK with it and just glad we caught the suspect.

* * * * *

It goes without saying that this job can land you in some extremely crazy and awkward moments as well, most of which are somewhat comical. It's not uncommon for example to respond to a residence and have someone come to the door that is either partially or fully naked. And it's always the people you do not want to see that like.

One night we were sent into a busy retail complex looking for a bunch of naked guys reported to be seen running up the road and behind stores and restaurants. Eventually we located the two of them behind a trash receptacle. One of them was wearing a foam restaurant to-go container taped over his junk, and the other was wearing a sock over his. Both of them had been digging through the trash in a desperate attempt to cover themselves. After speaking to them, it turns out that they were from a college in the city, and they had been blindfolded and dropped off naked as part of a fraternity initiation. While I found their misfortune hysterical, the state trooper and neighboring town cop I was with were not amused. In fact, they were threatening to arrest the students for charges of indecent exposure.

On top of the nudity you have to, of course, listen to all the crazy things that come out of some people's mouths. I will loop them into the "too much information" (TMI) category. This usually consists of someone telling you some bit of information during a call that is way too person and totally unnecessary to their story. Oftentimes, this cringe-worthy information injected into their story might contain something about their bowel movements or even their personal sex life and habits, which could have very easily been omitted. The difficult and funny part is not to laugh in their face when they are telling you such things or even break in your expression when they are talking. What I have found, however, is that some of these people aren't even ashamed and find nothing wrong with sharing this information.

When I was the Elderly Affairs advocate before I left on leave, I would sit in on meetings and do house visits to certain elderly people that may have needed assistance. One time I was in a meeting with several town officials with an elderly woman we were trying to get help for. Her husband had passed away recently, and when responders arrived on scene, they saw that the house was in deplorable conditions. The town ended up condemning the residence, and in the meeting we were trying to get her to take some of our assistance in cleaning the residence. The woman was very upset over the idea of someone going through her belongings, as most hoarders are. She kept bringing up her underwear drawer in particular, but what stopped everyone was the "photo album" she was concerned about people seeing.

Although we dismissed this, unsure what she was getting at, we assured her no one would be looking at her personal things. The woman then says, "You know, my photo album … umm, I was married over twenty years, and my husband was kinky." She probably detected the look on everyone's faces, because she said, "Doesn't everyone have one?" She then says, "Let me show you what we were all about" and pulls out an eight-by-ten picture of them both wearing medieval clothing (thank God) and holding swords.

Now mind you, the building inspector and two nice ladies from the department of Elderly Affairs are sitting at the table with me, and everyone has this disgusted look on their faces. Again, there are some personal details we just don't need to know.

I am not trying to ridicule God's children, but the way some of them live and act is just plain weird and disgusting. Take hygiene, for example. You would think it's a basic concept—you really don't need to have a lot of money to practice hygiene, unless, of course, you are homeless and do not have access to it.

I have been amazed at how some people live. I've seen houses where bowls of cereal and other foods are piled in the sink and have grown layers of mold over the top. Some have clothes scattered all over the floor, flattened as if they have been walked over for years, becoming almost like wallpaper against the floor. The worst thing, however, is dog and cat feces in people's houses. What makes you think it's OK to let your animals defecate on the floor for one, and not clean it up? These things that I am telling you about are not isolated incidents either but rather common issues I've have seen in multiple homes. I always find it funny when the owners of these houses will say, "Oh, excuse the mess" as if they just had some tidying up to do from the day before. Again, I am not trying to ridicule these people, but when you see how some other people live out there, it is downright scary. And some of these people live this way by choice.

This chapter was meant just to add a little more lightheartedness to this book and for me to also remember some of the calls I've been on. At the same token, I want to also accurately illustrate what this job is like so you may have a better overall understanding of it when we get to the following chapters.

* * * * *

PART II

* * * * *

Part II will begin to dive deeper into the cause and darkness that led to my PTSD. I need to warn you that from here on out, things are going to start getting very graphic as I make my way through some of this. I apologize in advance, but I must be as descriptive as possible to help get it out. What follows in the coming chapters is a series of events and stories to illustrate life as a cop. Please remember this book was as much a form of therapy for me during the healing process as it is meant to provide insight and awareness for you.

CHAPTER 9

AMID <u>THE</u> ENEMY: SUBSTANCE ABUSE, DEPRESSION, MENTAL HEALTH, <u>AND</u> EVIL

We know that we are the children of God and that the world around us is under the control of the evil one.
1 JOHN 5:19

Nobody can attest to evil in the world greater than police officers. We often see evil in some form almost on a daily basis, but not everyone recognizes it as such. I've dealt with many people who, I would argue, are being tormented by evil spirits. Spirits of anxiety and depression are not of God. Even though I myself am also struggling with such attacks from the enemy during my journey with PTSD, at least I am aware of what it is. This is why the devil is referred to in Christian circles as "the enemy."

Unfortunately not everyone recognizes this. I was once talking to someone, and I mentioned fear as being a weapon of the enemy, and she responded, "What enemy?" There is a lot of naivety about the devil among most worldly people—and even some Christians—as he is often painted as some fictitious cartoon character.

Chinese philosopher Sun Tzu, in The Art of War, says to "know your enemy, and know yourself, and you will win a hundred battles." This is very true; as a former military officer and now tactics instructor, I know that you can't defeat an enemy if you do not know their tactics. A lot of people want to blame crime and acts of violence on solely mental illness or circumstances of upbringing and living conditions. I would have to disagree. These things merely make way for evil to invade, and if you don't recognize this, then you become much more susceptible to attack.

At the onset of my PTSD, I could have easily fallen into the deep darkness of anxiety and depression, and I can now see how a lot of people do. Prior to PTSD, anxiety and depression were just meaningless words to me. I did not understand them, nor did I understand people who had them. I thought that these people were just weak or "messed up" in the head. I thought those people were just mentally ill or their surroundings and upbringings had led them through a mix of poor choices and lifestyle. In some cases, people develop anxiety and depression for various reasons; however, my recent experience has taught me that these conditions are no doubt part of a vicious attack by the enemy.

My mother recently said that we have only half of a chance without God. The enemy attacks everyone, even Christians, but it is much easier for him to attack non-believers and win. The enemy wins when people commit suicide, fall into a psychosis, or act out in violence (as is the case with active shooters). The enemy wins when people with anxiety and depression turn to substances to deal with their attacks. The problem is that most people do not recognize that clinically diagnosed disorders can also be accompanied with attacks by the enemy.

I have seen many people in very bad places in their lives. Police often get called to help these people, who have either attempted suicide or made threats to. People in these tough situations may overdose on medication, drugs, or alcohol. While some people will inherit problems of mental health and substance abuse by genetic disposition, this evil can also come from other family members and through what we allow into our house and what our children are exposed to. This brings up the old argument of nature versus nurture. I believe this also holds truth with household exposure to evil.

* * * * *

As cops, we often come across families that go through generational problems. We initially deal with the parents, then years later when their kids grow up, we begin dealing with the younger generation for some of the very same reasons. It's so sad to see people who feel there is no other option but death when they reach a certain state of depression and/or anxiety.

Many suicides take place in the home with family members around to discover the remains of the body. This has always boggled my mind, as I wondered how someone can be so selfish when committing suicide to leave the gruesome scene behind for surviving family members to suffer with. The problem is that depression and suicidal thoughts are often very selfish in nature, and the person is so consumed at the moment with their darkness that they are not thinking about anyone else but themselves. They are not thinking about the impact on their children, their spouse, or even the first responders who find them. What else could drive someone to that level but a real demonic influence?

I can recall a few specific incidents where I have personally seen demons fully manifested in people. I'll never forget a call we received for a manic individual walking along the road, screaming and shouting. We ended up having to wrestle him to ground to get him onto the rescue stretcher. Then, after struggling to strap him down, we had to handcuff him to the railings of the stretcher. The whole time, he was foaming at the mouth and sweating profusely.

At one point, he looked at me with this outer worldly glare and said in a raspy, creepy monster voice, "I'LL KILL YOU AND YOUR FAMILY ... AND BRING YOU TO HELL!"

I felt like he was looking directly into me; it was very frightening. That day, I saw a demon—not a man. Whatever was causing his hysteria, be it drugs or something else, there was no doubt the enemy was in full control at this point and even talking through him.

I've seen a few situations where people in some form of violent hysteria even start shouting out random things about spirits and condemning God. I can tell you this can be truly frightening, and while most people will chalk this kind of hysteria off as a reaction to drugs or excited delirium, you cannot help but see the evil behind it. There just seems to be a trend with this kind of behavior and some of the things that come out of the mouths of people in this state.

One day, we had a guy who was in the middle of the road causing all kinds of disturbance with traffic, claiming to be God and saying all kinds of bizarre things. I find it very interesting why people like this will often speak about God in such a manner unless there is a demon behind their behavior.

From my experience, evil doesn't discriminate by age either. This is very apparent by all the juvenile dealings we have that involve drugs and depression. It's not uncommon to find children who are "cutters" who have a habit of inflicting several cuts on themselves—not as a means of suicide but instead as a form of coping. I've dealt with suicidal children as young as eleven years old who have expressed to their friends that they plan to commit suicide. I had another child around the same age who had made statements of an intention to shoot up his school.

The enemy is relentless, and this is why I have come to believe it is important especially in today's secular world to start them early on to God, as they will be exposed to much evil sentiment in the world, which is now being accepted as commonplace in our culture. In the Gospels, Jesus talks about the innocence of children and encourages us to be more like them in our ways. Do not invite the enemy in your children's lives before they even have the chance to fight against it themselves. Parental actions can play a major role on the spiritual safety of a child.

We started dealing with a particular young child in our town at a very early age. This child was adopted, and we were told that his paternal parents practiced voodoo on him when he was a small child, placing him in a boiling pot of water as some part of a sick ritual before he was removed from them and placed in the custody of the state. This poor kid is no doubt suffering from a generation demon, stemming from the evil his parents engaged in. Very frequently he gets violently out of control and foams at the mouth, and we have to restrain him and send him to the hospital. He was so out of control once he began grabbing the furniture around him and hitting us with it. When we go to the house, we often have to restrain him while one of his parents forces liquid medicine up his nose, a sad scene that usually causes his nose to bleed. This child also suffers from chronic nerve pain in his arms as a reminder of his parents' satanic actions when he was a very small child. I truly do feel for this kid, and I fear as he gets older he will be a real danger to society if more intervention does not take place.

* * * * *

The enemy thrives on misfortune. When people get desperate, this is when they turn to darkness. Crime is often a result of desperation, and it is directly related to substance abuse. These are all the things of the devil's worldly playground. He knows that drugs lead to crime and violence; anxiety and depression to substance abuse and suicide. He does not want you to recover; he takes pleasure in the ways of the world and having his forces finding places to take space.

In John 12:31, Jesus calls Satan "the ruler of this world." The enemy thrives on the very human things we suffer, and there is so much of it here on earth. I have no doubt that I am under attack at times, but I must continue to resist and fight back, turning toward God. God seems to always come to people at times of trouble, as perhaps this is when he has the best opportunity to reach us. During times of trouble we tend to come to a fork in the road where we can either take the path of light or darkness, but sometimes the enemy can confuse us and we may be unsure which is which. The Bible tells darkness can be disguised as light: "And no wonder, for Satan himself masquerades as an angel of light" (2 Corinthians 11:14 NIV).

We have to be very careful when making decisions; I have seen a lot of people make poor judgement calls that have ended with them in prison or, worse, dead. Suicide, for example, is a decision, and some people believe that suicide is the ultimate freedom from their suffering. They believe their death will remove the burden of their problems from their loved ones. The enemy has lied to them and made them think that no one cares about them and the world would be better off without them. Like I mentioned earlier, suicides take a toll on everyone involved. Sometimes it is just a cry for help, but most of the time, it is a desperate attempt to end the suffering from dwelling in the darkness.

Every year around the holidays we would start to see an increase in the number of calls for suicidal threats, acts, and overdoses. It's interesting that Christmas, a time to celebrate Christ's coming to this world, is often a dark time for a lot of people. While Christmastime brings joy to most people, people suffering from depression tend to get much worse. I have heard a lot of depressed people tell me that Christmas is a difficult time of year for them. While most people are surrounded by family and joyous celebrations, this time often reminds people of the suffering and darkness of their own problems. All the positivity of Christmastime with the music and imagery tends to have the opposite effect on them, as if happiness were being thrown in their face.

> *"You intended to harm me, but God is intended for good to accomplish what is now being done, the saving of many lives."*
> GENESIS 50:20 NIV

In my twelve years of being a cop, I have seen a lot of suicides and death, which have been a main contributing factor to my own darkness. The enemy knows what images bother me and has exploited them into fear and worry, both mentally and physically. No bother, because I believe this is truly playing out to my advantage, or else I wouldn't have authored this book. Writing Invisible Wounds gave me a chance to look back to a few instances where I was able to stop someone in the middle of committing suicide. Talking about these things as I went along—logging these incidents away somewhere by putting them on paper and historicizing them—was a means of therapy.

It is common for us to get reports of concern from friends and family for suicidal individuals. People don't usually commit suicide in silence. I have found that they usually leave some sign or "tell" (either through text or social media) to friends and family. Oftentimes the sign is not something as direct as I am going to kill myself but rather a cryptic message that draws concern to people reading it. As much as someone wanting to commit suicide has reached the point of following through, usually some form of self-preservation kicks in, and they send a warning to others as a last cry for help. These types of calls will often come in as a well-being check from a friend or family member that the individual has said or done something concerning. Sometimes we are lucky enough to respond quickly enough to get to the person before they go through with it. However, on a few occasions, time was so imminent that I was the one to catch them in the act.

On one such call for a well-being check, I was walking around a residence, which was all locked up, when I peeked in the side garage window and saw the individual I was looking for slumped over in a chair with a generator running. This person was trying to kill himself with carbon monoxide poisoning—a successful method, and one I have seen work before. Unable to open the garage door, I smashed out the window with my expandable baton and was able to climb inside and open the garage and drag him outside to fresh air. While this man lived, I never knew what had happened to him or if he had ever tried to take his own life again.

Another time, I was responding to a residence for a well-being check when I located a vehicle in the driveway running with a dryer hose taped and sealed to the vehicle's exhaust and fed into the window, sealed with duct tape. The individual inside had the car running with all the doors locked and was slumped over the wheel. I immediately began ripping all of the hoses off, and we were eventually able to make entry into the vehicle by the windows.

One of the more memorable ones—and perhaps a main contribution to my PTSD—happened during one winter night. We had received a call for a suicidal male believed to be armed with a firearm that had been reported missing by his family. The dispatcher had conducted a GPS track of the person's cell phone through his wireless phone carrier and found a general location where he might have been. The location was pinged just over into the next town, and I happened to be not too far from the town line.

It was nighttime and cold with a previous snowfall on the ground. I radioed to dispatch I would attempt to locate the vehicle, then pulled down the road, which is void of any street lights and mostly barren as it borders some sandpits. That's when I came across his white pickup truck. As I pulled up, I activated my takedown lights and shined my spot into the cab of the truck. Due to the information I received that he was armed, I started doing a felony traffic stop and drew my firearm, aiming at the vehicle.

I could see the person's head moving about in the vehicle and suddenly saw him duck down, followed what I would describe as a plume of smoke or mist. I never actually heard the shot go off but suspected that was what happened. A few moments later, an officer from that town had pulled up next to me, and we began trying to order the person out of the vehicle. At some point, the driver door finally opened up and the individual just spilled out onto the ground next to it.

The other officer and I slowly approached with guns drawn.

What I saw next was completely horrifying. The bright-red tissue of this man's face was completely mangled. The lower half of his face, to include his mouth and jaw, was completely blown off with some freshly mangled, sagging flesh still hanging off the side of his head like torn paper.

As we drew near to him, the other officer shouted in horror, "He's still alive!"

The man was moving and twitching around on the ground like an injured animal that had been struck by a passing car. His eyes remained closed, and he wasn't even making a sound. No scream of pain, no moaning—just silence and slow movement.

I can't even imagine his state of mind at that point—if he was actually conscious enough to have one at that moment. Seeing him lying there not really dead and not really alive, I felt this strange and overwhelming urge to shoot him right then and there so he could just die and end his suffering.

This poor individual had taken a twelve-gauge shotgun loaded with buckshot to the face. The wadding from the shotgun round was still stuck in the headliner of the door of the truck. Strangely enough, I then knew that I saw the shot go off from behind the car, but I never heard it. They say in these circumstances that sometimes reality can seem altered, or in slow motion. Fight or flight is often referred to as the body's reaction to stressful situations, especially life-or-death ones. Combat-related stress can do weird things to the body, to include auditory exclusion (not hearing sound) and narrowing of vision (tunnel vision).

On a side note: Combat stress has been studied for decades, and we know fear is a main part of it. If any cop ever tells you that he has never been afraid, then he is lying to you and himself. Fear is only natural in this job, violence and danger are not normal to the human body, but cops are continuously exposed to it. On this call, a variety of things could have gone differently. People who are suicidal and armed have sometimes resorted to the police to end their life. This is known as suicide by cop. I knew this person was armed and really had no idea of whether his intentions were to harm me or not.

In the police academy you learn about the Stress Arousal Color Code, developed by Jeff Cooper in Principals of Personal Defense.2 This code is based on different levels of stress arousal and heartrate. At home, you may be in a white zone, which is relaxed in your boxers on the sofa. On your way into to work, you could be in condition yellow. There have been studies conducted with first responders wearing heart monitors, which showed heightened heart rates at various stages of the day, to include the ride into work. In condition orange, you may have heightened senses and on the defensive or very alert. This is most likely where most police officers spend their day during a shift. If a cop is in condition white on duty, then he has become too compliant and is a danger to himself. In the red condition, you start to enter that action or "fight or flight" mode and your body is getting ready to run or fight.

Later on, famous combat psychology writer, Lt. Col. Dave Grossman, founder of Killology Research Group and author of On Combat and On Killing, added two more conditions to the arousal code: gray and black. In these two conditions Grossman states that our physical and cognitive functions start to degrade rapidly. According to Grossman, it is possible to still be functional in the gray zone; however, the one condition you don't want to be in is black. Black means panic has set in and taken control, and the body is now shutting down instead of trying to survive. Cops that

---

2. Jeff Cooper, *Principals of Personal Defense* (Paladin Press, 2006).

have gone in black zone often get injured or, worse, killed.

Getting back to the call …

The rescue workers had finally showed up on scene, which seemed to take forever, and they were pretty much useless anyway. It's not really their fault, though. How do you help someone like this? His face is blown off.

Wait a minute, let me go grab some gauze and Band-Aids from my trunk. There we go, that's better.

I'll never forget the firefighters staring at him in disbelief, like they did not even know what to do.

One of them asked me to shine my flashlight on his gear bag so he could see what he was doing.

Moments later, he had moved the bag, but I must have been still standing there holding the light on the empty spot on the ground, apparently in shock, because someone tapped me on the shoulder and asked me if I was OK.

The rescue workers lowered the stretcher to the ground, and they placed a backboard on top of the stretcher. For some reason, they forgot to strap him onto the backboard, so when they raised the stretcher, he flopped right off the stretcher and headfirst into the snow-covered ground.

Standing there shocked, I winced as they lifted him up off the ground and his bloody mangled face left a red imprint in the snow below.

When I got back to the station, I began typing my report, and one of the officers who was on the peer support team came in and handed me a sheet of paper on PTSD. He asked me if I was all right and told me to read the paper, and that was the only extent of debriefing I ever received. This was also the last time anyone from peer support was ever offered to me in the remainder of my twelve years.

A few days later, I was driving into work at night and saw an oncoming vehicle with a smashed-up front end and missing headlight. I immediately went back to the image of the man's mangled face in my mind. It was at this point that I realized how similar vehicles' front ends are to human faces. I later learned cars were designed this way on purpose, but I'll never forget that reaction. I had mentioned it to a few people, but nothing was ever really done about it. As with every other traumatic experience cops see, we bury it, maybe make light of it, and press on.

For years I never knew what happened to this fellow, but I learned that he did survive and was still very depressed. However, within the last few years he had come to the police station and was looking to talk to the officer who responded that night. I met with him and was surprised to see how good he looked. Minus a section of a skin graft on his face, he looked pretty good. He told me that they were able to take some bone and reconstruct a jaw and mouth. You could tell his tongue was still messed up and his speech was not the best, but still he looked great. The gentleman then went on to to express to me how thankful he was for me saving his life.

Surprised, I said, "I didn't save your life," to which he replied, "Yeah, you did. By you pulling up behind me, I got nervous, and hurrying, I slipped with the shotgun." The man went on to ask me, "Was that you who stood on the bumper of my car?"

I said, "No, nobody stood on the bumper of your car."

But he seemed convinced that someone was standing on the car when he shot himself. He was more than convinced there was someone there with him. I can't help but wonder if maybe it was an angel—who knows. But he seemed comforted by its presence.

I was able to get some closure after speaking with him. Most of the time, we see people in traumatic events and send them off to the hospital, and we never know what happens to them. Sometimes we are required to place a call to the emergency room to see if that person has passed, but other than that, most incidents go without any kind of closure for the first responder.

This is the first real incident I put on paper, so I was hoping to be able to lock it away or begin to anyway so I could move forward. I don't want to necessarily forget my career as a cop, but I need to process much of what I have seen in order to be healthy.

* * * * *

In the next chapter I'm going to shift for a little bit and talk about some incidents that, while not related to death and trauma, have taken a toll on me and I wanted to record. You see most of these incidents involved scary situations or circumstances that were close calls and stressful dangerous events that I have been talking to my clinician about. I've come to learn that PTSD is cumulative, and it also includes repeated exposure to danger as well as trauma. I believe these incidents have also contributed to my burnout and PTSD.

CHAPTER 10

"FIGHT OR FLIGHT": EFFECTS ON THE MIND AND BODY

Even though I walk through the valley of the shadow of death, I will fear no evil.
PSALM 23:4 ESV

In the previous chapter I started to talk about fear and the body's reaction to combat and stress. Although we are not soldiers, cops are placed in dangerous scenarios on a daily basis across the nation. At any second, any call or traffic stop can go really bad. If this was a safe job, then we wouldn't have to strap on body armor and a gun every day.

Being a firearms instructor, I have learned that cops fall into various categories. Some feel they may never have to engage someone in a fire fight; others, like myself, like to train to be proficient for the worst-case scenario. I've always found that the people who were not "gun guys" lived in a bubble of complacency, believing something like that would never happen to them, and if it did, they would just deal with it then.

I've had guys tell me, "No training can prepare you for the real thing. You just act."

OK, to some extent that is true: When "it" hits the fan, you are just going to react or not react. Training, however, does give you a baseline. If you are more proficient with a firearm, for exam-

114

ple, you have a better chance of surviving a gun battle.

Even though I am now in a position of weakness from my PTSD, I can honestly say although I feared death in an unhealthy way, I did not fear a fire fight as much, because I felt there was a level of control I had. Being a firearms instructor, among other trainings and certifications, I felt that I was the best prepared I could be for anything that came my way. What I did not feel comfortable with was dying from a random illness or tragedy such as a heart attack or car accident. That same fear extends to my family and loved ones. I fear most what I cannot control. What I have learned through this journey is that fear is a powerful weapon of the enemy.

> *For God has not given us a spirit of fear, but of power and of love and of a sound mind.*
> 2 TIMOTHY 1 : 7 NKJV

Fear, however, is the context of law enforcement is also a necessary evil. When in a dangerous situation on a call, it is perfectly normal to be afraid, but it does take a toll on you. While writing this book, I found myself looking back on many of my calls through my time in psychotherapy, and I couldn't help but think of all the times things could have gone really bad. It's scary to think that on some of these calls, I could have been seriously injured or killed.

I'm going to go out on a limb here and say that the average person has never experienced real life-threatening fear from violence or exposure to trauma—this fear that they could soon die as they step foot somewhere. The level at which police officers experience trauma during their time as a cop is astronomically high.

According to one estimate, a police officer could experience somewhere upwards of nine hundred traumatic incidents during their time on duty.3 This real fear of death and trauma is faced by first responders repeatedly, and it wears on the mind and body. The fear is even greater if you have family that you care for, because your safety is not just about just you anymore.

Imagine yourself for a minute being a firefighter and heading into a burning structure. This is your job; you have been trained in all the right ways to be as safe as possible. Yet at any moment, you may become trapped or crushed by falling debris.

Now imagine you are a police officer being dispatched to a domestic disturbance. The dispatcher tells you one of the individuals is armed with large kitchen knife. You may be the first and only person on scene and will have to make a life or death decision.

If you are a cop reading this, you know the feeling I am talking about—the feeling you get when you're sitting in your cruiser and you hear the dispatcher say one of those trigger words (knife, gun, or weapon). Upon hearing this, you peel out from where you are parked, flying down the road, and your heart feels like it drops for a second right before it goes into overdrive. You really don't have time to process the danger completely because you are trying to get to the call. You may start playing things out in your head. I used to find myself trying to calm myself and control my heart rate by the time I got to the scene. After all, this is your job, you cannot run away and hide. You aren't dialing 911; you are 911.

Cops can even gauge the severity of the call just by the

3. D. Rudofossi, *A Cop Doc's Guide to Public Safety Complex Trauma Syndrome: Using Five Personality Styles (Death, Value, and Meaning)* (Amityville, NY: Baywood Publishing Company, 2009).

inflection in the dispatcher's voice when they start calling badge numbers. A good indicator of a hot call is usually when the dispatcher starts calling three or more badges over the radio, or when they frantically say something like, "I NEED CARS TO START HEADING TO …" When you hear this, it means, Just start going that way, more information to follow. This can really start getting your blood pumping. Chances are when you hear this, you know it's bad.

Racing to the call, in the back of your mind you know that if there is a chance you might have to shoot someone, then you will be subject to court trial as a murder suspect and the next headline in the news. You could be sued or, worse, put in jail, depending how a jury of "your peers" (civilians) decide your fate on a world they do not understand.

You will often hear officers in shooting investigations use the defense that "they were in fear for their lives." The problem is, unless you were in their shoes, how does anyone know what that fear felt like? Someone sitting on a jury who has never been a cop cannot possibly relate to that. This is why I am never too quick to judge any officer-involved shooting I see on the news. I have been there; I know that feeling of fear. But most people don't and never will.

* * * * *

I can remember the first time I actually felt an overwhelming fear accompanied by the thought that I could die. I was recently off of FTO and was on my first year of probation. Still very new to the job, I was dispatched, along with my academy mate and the shift sergeant, to call involving a suicidal male. I was on second shift at the time, and the call had come in around ten thirty at night. The dispatcher advised us that the wife had called 911 and reported that her husband was armed with a shotgun in their bedroom and was threatening to kill himself. The wife said that her husband was unaware she was on the phone with 911 and she was going to meet us at the bottom of the street.

As we pulled down the street, we parked down the road away from the house. The house was at the top of a hill, over a wide stretch of open lawn. We met with the wife, and the sergeant had her explain the layout of the house to us. The wife told us that upon entering the house, there was a stairwell directly across from the front door leading to the upstairs. She told us that her bedroom was on the left at the top of the stairs and her husband was sitting on the edge of the bed, facing the door with his shotgun.

I remember standing there in the dark looking at my buddy, also brand-new, and could read the same expression on his face. Of course, being on the job like a day, we were looking to the sergeant for what to do.

So they will probably try to call him and negotiate him out of the house somehow.

I was surprised, however, when the sergeant unholstered his gun and said, "You guys ready to do this?"

Following his lead, my buddy and I unholstered our weapons and began following him up the hill across the lawn. My first thought was, Oh my God, this is it. I'm going to die here. I then thought that I didn't even get to say bye to my wife.

As we crossed the lawn in the moonlight, I could see the light glowing from the top bedroom window, and my mind began to race. My life at that moment literally flashed before my eyes as I began to think of this individual pumping off shotgun rounds at us as we entered the house. I saw myself as the father of children for the first time, my wife and me in our old age, and how I might never experience any of those things.

We got the door of the house and stacked on the exterior wall.

The sergeant said, "Straight up the stairs, don't stop. Ready?"

At this point, I didn't have time to think any more about my future—it was go time.

We opened the door, then rushed up the stairs, and the next thing I remember was tackling the husband on the bed and handcuffing him. Sure enough, he was there, with a shotgun, sitting on the edge of the bed, but we had completely caught him off guard.

Afterward, I called my wife and my mother at the time to tell them what had happened.

I think over the years my mother lived in a lot of denial about the true nature and danger of my job. I knew that she never really liked it, but I think it gave her a false sense of security to think that things like this never really happened, or maybe she even played down the seriousness about them in her own mind. It wasn't until a journalist of local newspaper years later snapped a picture of me wearing tactical body armor and holding a rifle during a standoff with an armed suspect that she said reality had hit her. I remember her getting upset with the photograph and me saying, "Mom, what did you think I did for a job?"

I guess in every mother's head is the image of a police officer in a crisp uniform, just driving around during the day. While this is probably about 90 percent true, there are many moments like the one I just described that will happen over the course of a career in law enforcement.

I'm going to be honest myself and say that before that call, I too really did not think I would be doing things like that. I know you train for the extreme in the academy, but I really did not think those things actually happened (or at least not in the town I was going to be working for).

* * * * *

Several years later, we got a similar call. This time, however, it was for a disturbance. The caller told 911 that her ex-son-in-law had forced entry into her house and was arguing with her daughter. While on the phone with the 911 dispatcher, she said he grabbed box of ammunition and went upstairs to retrieve a rifle, threatening to kill them and any police who arrived on scene.

Let me tell you, hearing this information over the radio while going to this call was a real pucker factor. The caller and her daughter were able to escape the house, advising he was now armed with a high-powered rifle and infrared scope. She told the dispatcher that he said, "When the cops get here, there is going to be a blood bath."

Now, being from the military, I know that infrared means that the scope allows someone to see heat signatures in the dark. These are commonly used for hunting as well. If you have ever seen the movie Predator, that will give you an idea of what infrared is all about. My main concern was that although it was dark out, this individual could see our movement through his scope.

After parking down the road, we geared up with our rifles. Again, it was me, my academy mate, and this time another officer and sergeant. Being from the military as well and having served in Iraq, my buddy suggested someone take a first aid kit with us. I said, "Good idea" and started looking through the issued first aid kits we had in the trunks.

The kits looked ancient and pristine, as if no one had ever

touched them. All they had in them were mini gauze packs, rolls, Band-Aids, and rubber gloves—pretty much all useless if you are shot with a high-powered hunting rifle.

This moment actually changed a lot for me, as after this I dedicated myself to helping officers in my department become trained and equipped in managing gunshot wounds just the way the military does. I paid my own way, eight hundred dollars, to become certified as an instructor for Officer Down Rescue and got trained as a Tactical Emergency Medical Specialist. Tactical Emergency Casualty Care (TECC) has become huge in the first responder world since the Boston Marathon Bombing, and with the rise of active shooter incidents, many departments are now training in it. But like all police trainings in departments, they are typically reactive and not proactive and open to new things. The "until it happens here" mentality is usually the reasoning, due to limited training budgets in municipalities.

Grabbing our useless medical bag and securing rifles from the trunk, I made the mistake of calling my wife before we headed out. The phone call was very quick because we were just about to step off. The call went something like this: "Hey, I can't talk, but I'm about to go on a really dangerous call, pray for me, bye." (To my wife, if you are reading this, I am still very sorry, and I wasn't thinking about the mental state you would be in after I hung up waiting to hear my call back that I was OK.)

It was pretty dark out at the time, and the house faced the main road, so we decided to head farther down the road and cut into the woods and approach the house from behind. The whole time, I can picture myself in the crosshairs of an infrared rifle scope as I dart from tree to tree for cover, trying to stay as low to the ground as possible. My other military buddy is doing the same. The other two officers, neither of whom had served in the military, were walking rather nonchalantly along out in the open and had lost sight of me, as I was hugging the ground behind a tree.

As a tactical trainer, I later realized that simple combat concepts taught in the Army, such as cover and concealment, were not something most police officers were familiar with. I later made a point to integrate moving from cover to cover in buddy teams during future firearms trainings. There is still a large gap with tactical training and law enforcement. Unless you belong to a specialized unit such as SWAT, most officers lack the proper skills and knowledge for advanced high-risk scenarios. There is also a stubborn reluctance to bring these skills down to regular patrol officers, as the mentality seems to be, That's a SWAT thing.

Well, clearly it's not, as I have gone on many of these calls while working patrol, and survival is not just "a SWAT thing." I have always made it a point as an instructor—whether in tactical medicine, firearms, or active shooter training—to bridge the gap between SWAT and patrol. You see, in most departments SWAT is useless. Most critical incidents just unfold too fast, and patrol officers are always the first on scene dealing with them. Most SWAT teams are part time, underfunded, and undertrained. Not to mention it takes an act of God to activate them.

There is a high liability associated with calling out a SWAT team. The whole process usually involves some sort of command decision process, and then phone calls have to be placed to order people into the scene. Most of the time, the scene is over and done with by then. Especially in the age of so many active shooter incidents, the standard protocol across the country now is that patrol no longer waits for SWAT to arrive on scene.

This is why so many people perished in the Columbine

incident. At the time, patrol officers were instructed to set up a perimeter and contain. During Columbine, there was a large presence of police officers on scene within a matter of minutes; however, none of them entered the school, because that's how they were trained. Officers responding to active shooter incident are now trained to make entry and eliminate the threat, even if only one officer arrives on scene first. Time equals lives, and you have a gun, so get in there and use it.

Don't get me wrong, SWAT has its place in major metro areas, where they are full-time teams serving high-risk warrants, but for the most part, I think they are obsolete in our current day and age, especially since many smaller departments don't even have access to such resources. Instead, all police departments should be moving toward tactical patrol and outfitting, along with training every officer in high-risk scenarios.

Getting back to the call …

We made our way through the dark woods to the backyard of the house, toward an additional rental house, which we had to sneak around. At the same time, we had to secretly evacuate the residences in case the bullets started flying. The dispatcher was able to make contact on the phone with the suspect and had him come to the rear window. The guy came to the window of the kitchen, where he was faced with the bright flashlights attached to the end of several rifles. We had him put both arms out the window, then we yanked him out of the window onto the ground, where he was cuffed without incident. I and two other officers then did a sweep of the house to make sure no one else was in there and to seize the weapons. Although this is another call that ended peacefully, it could have gone so much differently.

* * * * *

Years later we had a standoff with another guy who was armed and was holding his sister in the house with him. This was actually our second standoff with this guy. The first one had gone overnight, and this second one lasted three full days. The state police SWAT and our local team were called out, along with members of the state bomb squad. During the incident, we had time to use such resources as SWAT, as the individual had barricaded himself, and I was one of the initial responding officers.

At the scene we discovered that the guy had lined his yard and windows with propane canisters meant to be traps, I guess. Although the bomb technician did not believe that shooting propane canisters would be a threat, we proceeded with caution anyway. I ended up walking through the woods around the house with a state trooper, and we set up a perimeter around the house. The individual inside was armed with a shotgun and yelling at us from inside the house.

From my location at the rear right corner of the house, I could see the door to the back porch and was facing two sets of windows. We were able to make contact with the sister from the back porch and had her come where I was. As she came outside, I had to expose myself from cover to meet her halfway. Wondering when I was going to catch a round, I started yelling for her to run toward me. It's in these moments that you realize your safety could be in serious jeopardy and you just don't know. I would always pray for safety and hope God was listening.

This individual was seriously troubled, and they ended up launching a ton of CS tear gas into his house, which had no effect on him. At one point he even shot off a few rounds toward the area of the front of the house where officers were hiding behind a berm.

After the state police SWAT team literally tore the front and both sides of his house off with an armored vehicle ram, he finally gave up, seventy hours later. That first day, though, I lay on the cold wet ground behind a rifle for approximately eight hours before I was eventually relieved by other officers.

I've been involved in a few standoffs, and the suspect always knows he has the upper hand and time is on his side. Most agencies are not willing to make entries on armed suspects, as they don't want to put everyone at stake in danger, and usually time is the only factor at play. Usually the key to winning standoffs is just waiting the individual out.

I was in another standoff in an apartment building with a frequent troublemaker who claimed he had a firearm on the other side of his apartment door. For the duration of the standoff, which lasted four hours, I was standing in a hallway in a stack of guys, just waiting to make entry. We had to wake up everyone in the apartment building and evacuate them outside.

I knew the guy was full of crap, and we had the ballistic shield. I kept saying, "Screw it, let's just boot the door in and end this." I was even willing to go first, as I was the only officer who had a heavier duty tactical body armor over my uniform. Unfortunately, they chose to activate the Sit Wait and Talk Team (SWAT for short), who also just stood there collecting overtime and wouldn't make entry. He eventually agreed to come out, and my instincts were right—he didn't even have a firearm. But we can't always take that chance.

* * * * *

Last year sometime, I was responding to a 911 hang-up call. These happen all the time, and 99 percent of the time they are accidental—a child or an elderly person misdialed.

So I headed to this call, and when I pull up to the house, I recognize it as a trouble house that belongs to a problem family we deal with a lot. The father is always drunk, the older son did time in jail for pulling a knife on some kids behind one of our businesses, and the youngest son was now out of high school and onto his career of choice dealing drugs. My backup at this point is the shift lieutenant, who is still on his way from the other side of town.

As I walk up to the residence, the father opens the door. "It's Jacob," he says. "He's in his room out of control."

I immediately radio in the disturbance, then proceed to the bedroom.

The door is locked, and I can hear Jacob yelling and banging things around.

"Jacob, what's going on, man?" I say. "Can you unlock the door for me?"

"I WANT TO [explicit] DIE. JUST SHOOT ME!" Jacob yells back.

"Jake, I don't want to shoot you, man. Just unlock the door for me."

All of a sudden, I hear the distinctive click of the door lock popping open. I open the door, and standing a few feet away is Jacob—shirtless, sweating profusely, and holding a large heavy bedpost as a weapon, torqued up over his shoulder and ready to swing.

I drew my service weapon, yelled, "DROP IT!" and quickly radioed, "He's got a weapon, speed it up!"

Upon aiming my weapon at him, he angrily flings the bed post against the wall, then picks up his entire bed—mattress, box spring, and all—and flips it over.

I transition to my TASER weapon at this point and have it

down by my side.

Jacob then decides to charge me at the doorway, and I shoot him directly in the chest. He immediately drops to his side into the bedroom closet.

The father runs in the room and yells at him, "THAT'S WHAT YOU GET!"

Seconds later, the supervisor runs in and cuffs Jacob.

"I HATE YOU!" Jacob yells at his father. "THIS IS ALL YOUR FAULT. I JUST WANT TO DIE!"

Later, the lieutenant tells me as he was entering the house, he heard the pop of the TASER weapon and thought I had fired a shot at Jacob.

"I almost did," I say. "He wanted me to."

Turns out Jacob was high on "Molly" (ecstasy/MDMA) and crack cocaine, and I came close to maybe having to shoot him.

* * * * *

Coming close to killing someone is a very strange feeling. And there was one other specific time where I came even closer than the standoff with Jacob. We had responded to a residence for an unknown male armed with a knife. The neighbor had some concerns—she had not heard or seen the woman across the street—and when she went to go check on her, the husband grabbed a knife and scared her away.

When we got on scene, we saw a garage attached to the house and a door that led inside. As we approached the open garage, I considered my backup who were with me: a friend of mine (not really much of a good shot or tactical guy), his trainee recruit, and another guy who had only had about two years on the job. Considering their skill level, I decided to take the lead as the best trained officer on scene.

As we walked into the garage, I could hear the guy yelling from the other side of the door. I gently tried the door, which was locked, and told one of the other officers to have a TASER weapon for a less than lethal option. In situations like these, it's best to have deadly force (your firearm) ready, but if there are enough officers on scene, having a TASER weapon, for example, as an option may be a viable alternative to killing someone. TASER weapons are great, and they do save lives, but they should never be a substitute for a firearm in a deadly force encounter.

I tried talked to the guy on the other side of the door in my typical fashion.

"Hey, what's going on, man? Can we talk?"

Unfortunately, the only response I got from inside started with an expletive.

At this point I have no clue what this guy looks like or how old he is, but he sounds very angry and unstable. So I say, "Hey, are you alone in there?"

"NO! SHE [his wife] IS HERE AND YOU'RE NOT COMING IN!" he yells back.

"Look, guy, there's no need for all this. We just want to check on you guys."

"---- YOU!" he yells once again. "COME GET ME!"

Right then, a supervisor on scene gave me the signal to make entry. When I kicked the door in, I was shocked to see the suspect.

Standing only three to five feet away from me in the kitchen was a middle-aged man, most likely in his late fifties, wearing nothing but an adult diaper and holding a knife, which is pointing right at me. To confuse the issue even more, behind him is a wheelchair.

Now, this is a good time to point out to those who are most critical about police shootings what a split-second decision looks like. In this instance, my mind is quickly trying to process all this information and determine how much of a threat this guy is. Oh, and by the way, I am also worried about being stabbed at the same time.

Knives are very dangerous, and there is a general rule of thumb that you should have at least twenty feet or more in between you and someone with a knife for your reactionary safety. Someone close to you with a knife may be able to move quickly enough to injure you even before you are able enough to get a shot off or prevent being stabbed.

I immediately jump backward, literally bumping into the other officers behind me. While pointing my gun at the man, I yell, "DROP THE KNIFE!"

The guy then lunges forward as if to stab me and yells, "SHOOT ME!"

Now at this point, based on the short distance away and his aggressive advance toward me, I or anyone else there would have been justified to shoot him. For some reason, though, because of the diaper and wheelchair in the circumstances, I was questioning how mobile this guy was, and when he lunged a few steps forward, he stopped just short of me, which confirmed the fact that he just wanted me to shoot him.

Because he did not come any farther toward me in his lunge, I figured he was playing chicken and was hoping I or someone else would have shot him. (This is all unfolding very quickly, by the way.) With my gun still trained on him, I yell at the other officer, "Use your TASER weapon!"

The officer shoots his TASER weapon, but nothing happens

because only one TASER weapon probe makes contact (two have to hit the individual to complete a circuit).

So I yell, "HIT HIM AGAIN!"

The officer fires a second shot, and this time, the guy locks up and falls to the ground.

His poor wife—during this whole altercation—has been hiding, locked in the bedroom.

After the encounter, my buddy said, "That's the closest I ever came to shooting someone. When he came toward you, I had my finger on the trigger."

"Yeah, me too," I said, "but I didn't know how far he was going to advance and took a chance." If that had been anyone else, I would have shot them.

In those very few seconds all this unfolded, I made a judgement call based on what I had. On the one hand, I saw the diaper he was wearing and the wheelchair in the kitchen behind him, yet here he was standing very able in front of me, actually darting toward me with a knife. This judgement call could have gone both ways. Despite the diaper and wheelchair, we did confirm later that he was very mobile and several months prior had fought with an officer while the two tumbled down the basement stairs. Because of this, it was clear he was very capable of continuing forward and stabbing me, but I don't believe that was his goal—his goal was to move forward enough for me to shoot him. As I mentioned earlier, this is called suicide by cop.

Sorry, dude. Not today, I'm not giving you the satisfaction.

Now, of course there were other factors at play with this individual. It turns out he had a previous head injury, which affects controlling his bowel movements, which is why he wears a diaper. No doubt that this brain injury also caused his violent behavior.

The bottom line is, a lot of people police deal with have mental health issues of some kind, whether diagnosed or not. Sometimes these people become the victims of police shootings because they are armed and out of control. Unfortunately, when someone gets killed by the police like this, the public and family are naturally outraged, but how else are we as police officers supposed to deal with situations where people are armed with weapons? Our lives have value as well, and at the end of the day, I have a responsibility to go home to my family. In this situation, I made the decision not to shoot, but it could have easily resulted in me getting severely injured or killed.

Of course the next few days, we were ridiculed by other officers not on scene that day for using a TASER weapon on "an old guy wearing a diaper in a wheelchair." Yeah, that's not exactly the case, and all the officers on scene knew that, but this is the culture we live in. All the Type A people we talked about earlier will say how they would have done it better or that they "would have just tackled him."

Yeah, OK, hero. Let me see you run at someone and tackle them when they are pointing a large blade aggressively at you. It's easy for someone to criticize you after the fact when they weren't there. Cops love to puff themselves up and take credit away from others, even when they do a good job in a situation like that and no one gets hurt. After all, isn't that all that matters? Supervisors in general are especially critical of your actions, especially if they were not there to witness the event unfold.

CHAPTER 11

VICARIOUS TRAUMA THROUGH TRAUMA

Then Jesus said, "Come to me, all of you who are weary and carry heavy burdens, and I will give you rest."
MATTHEW 11:28

It's about to get a little graphic in this chapter. Again, I apologize for this, but in order for me to process these events, they must be detailed and written down. I suspect much like after therapy sessions, I may have some anxious moments and residual fallout later at night, but this is something I have become used to, and I believe it's all necessary for the healing process, for these are the burdens I carry. I am truly starting to believe that God has brought me here.

While I mentioned much earlier I do not believe fear and anxiety are from God, I do believe he uses such as an opportunity to bring us back to him from darkness in times of trouble. Proverbs 3:5 tells us, "Do not depend on your own understanding." We know God works in mysterious ways that we don't always have the ability to understand or see initially. Through God's given wisdom, eventually you will be led to understand your current trials and circumstance. God's ways are not your ways: "For My thoughts are not your thoughts, nor are your ways My ways" (Isaiah 55:8 NKJV).

"'For I know the plans I have for you,' declares the Lord, 'plans to prosper you and not to harm you, plans to give you hope and a future."
JEREMIAH 29:11 NIV

This is where I believe I am at during this point of uncertainty. Though I am still in limbo as of writing this, currently without pay and with an unknown future ahead of me, my family and I are starting to see some things come together. I am really starting to believe God does not want me in policing anymore. Now further along in this journey, I have come to realize that this job was not good for me mentally and spiritually. And yet, God had me perform the job, maybe to use some of my experience and skill elsewhere later on, or perhaps to even to call awareness to the issue of PTSD among first responders.

I do know one thing: I am a good public speaker and trainer, and I don't feel I was able to use these skills to my full potential where I was. I have this vision of a new job where I am teaching and presenting information to help others. Prior to my leave of absence, I began teaching emergency trauma training designed to help first responders and average citizens be able to respond and help in a critical scenario. I have since taught the entire department and various school teachers. My passion is teaching firearms and tactics, and ideally I am better suited somewhere else to help others, as my skills have not always been recognized in the past.

Each of you should use whatever gift you have received to serve others, as faithful stewards of God's grace in its various forms.
1 PETER 4:10 NIV

Again, my reading of the Scriptures confirms what I have been feeling. If you are new to reading the Bible, I suggest you start with all of Paul and Peter's letters as well as Proverbs and Psalms. I have found a lot of relevant information to our day and age, especially scriptures that I have felt speak to me directly.

I also feel that the environment I was in was not good for my spiritual growth. This is not only due to the atmosphere around co-workers but also all the tragedy and darkness I was constantly exposed to.

Death is not something anyone likes to talk about. Death and tragedy are things we as humans are only exposed to in relatively small doses and for the most part controlled circumstances. Someone you may know passes away, and you may have to view them in their coffin at a wake and attend a funeral, but most people do not see the raw, unedited version when it comes to the sequence and process of death.

As first responders, we are the first to arrive on scene when someone has either recently passed or has been deceased and is now going through the process of decaying. Death is the ugliest, worst thing I have seen, and having direct contact with the deceased as a part of my job led me to a state of fear, depression, and an overwhelming sense of looming tragedy.

Being a first responder in a place where someone's loved one has passed also exposes you to the grief and tragedy of the family as well. Even though these people are not known to you, how can you not feel their suffering and imagine it being your family? Again, this is not something I've had to witness just once in my lifetime but over and over again in this job.

I tell myself, *I have had enough, I can't see anyone dead anymore. I can't see any grieving family members and pain anymore to the level of exposure I have seen it.*

My clinician tells me that it is really all about perspective. She says, "If someone asks me if there was a lot of crime where I live, I would say no, but if someone asks you, you would say yes, but you are exposed to it."

This is why many cops sit with their backs to the wall at restaurants, distrust everyone, and scan the crowds everywhere they go. A cop's perspective of the world is vastly different than most of the public because of their exposure. The same scenario applies to my exposure to tragedy and death. Most people are not exposed to the same level of tragedy, illness, and death as first responders and emergency room staffs are. This is why I have come to fear that I have a greater chance of a tragedy happening in my personal life to me or my family: because I see it happen on a higher frequency than most people to others.

Now, there is no mistake that the enemy is at work here and has exploited this fear. I have come a long way in the process since the onset, but I still believe it is not his will for me to go back into that exposure.

I was never someone who liked gore or scary movies, and therefore it should have come as no surprise that I would be bothered by images of dead people throughout the years. These images bothered me for many reasons, but I will get more on that in the next chapter.

In the very beginning if anything, I was curious when going to these types of calls. There is always that feeling of, I don't want to look, but I can't stop looking. This is where things are going to start to get graphic, so again, I apologize.

* * * * *

I can remember my first deceased person call when I was brand-new. I remember that it was an elderly gentleman who had passed away in bed, and the family had found him the next morning. Now, you would think that this is an easy introduction to death. What better way to die than to die peacefully in your sleep right? Let me get this out of the way: There is no good way to die, and this call proved it to me right from the start.

This gentleman had something happen to him overnight—I don't even know what—but he had dried blood coming all out of his nose, and it was stuck on the pillow, and it was just gross. This doesn't say much for dying peacefully in one's sleep. The medical examiner on scene found out I was new and asked me if I wanted touch the body to feel the temperature and check for stiffness, I'm pretty sure I said, "I'll pass," and this was also my first experience being around grieving family members, with a loved one dead in the other room.

When people die, their body does a lot of things. Their bowels and bladder usually let go, making them urinate and defecate. Oftentimes they also aspirate, and fluid comes out of their mouth. There is no pretty way to die, sorry to break it to you, unless maybe you happen to be around during the rapture and Jesus just takes you up with him in the clouds (hopefully before the great tribulation).

When people die, there is a science that we use to determine how long they have been deceased. This is done by feeling the body for temperature and checking for things like lividity (blood settling) and rigor (stiffness). All these things can correspond to specific time frames of how long the person has been dead. The scary thing is that the body almost immediately begins the decaying process once blood stops pumping. If now more than anything, this is all the more reason to believe that the human body from the time of original sin is not perfect and merely a vessel for our real self and what makes up who we are in spirit and soul. At least this has helped me cope in the past with processing when people die.

"By the sweat of your brow you will eat your food until you return to the ground, since from it you were taken; for dust you are and to dust you will return" (Genesis 3:19 NIV).

When bodies start decaying, they begin to emit a very particular smell. Once you have ever smelled it, it's unmistakable and usually the first indication upon entering a residence that the person inside is dead. Sometimes you can even pick up the odor from the outside of the residence.

One time we were doing a well-being check of an older woman who had not been heard from in a while. The house was all locked up, and we had to force entry, but as we were standing outside, one of the fire department captains said, "Oh yeah, she's dead. I can already smell it." This smell lingers in your nostrils and sticks on your clothes if you are around it too long.

Well-being checks can go a few ways: Either the person is fine, not home, injured, or dead. On some occasions I have found people incapacitated because they had fallen and couldn't reach their phone, and thanks to nosy neighbors we were able to find them. Nobody likes the outcome of finding someone dead during a well-being check, because you just don't know how long they have been there.

Unfortunately for this poor woman, the fire captain was right. Upon entering the residence, I found a trail of what looked like dried diarrhea leading down the hallway, where I found her naked outside the bathroom. It appears this woman had some kind of stomach issue just prior to the moment of her death and had made

137

a really big mess in the house. I could see the areas of the dried diarrhea had swirl marks in them as if she had tried to wipe up the mess and possibly take a shower, but must have died in the process. This scene was disturbing indeed and one I will never forget. The scene I saw depicted a story of suffering to me. I could not help but imagine this poor woman not being able to control her bowel movements feeling very ill and alone and desperately trying to wipe it up moments before her death.

As a person, it's difficult for me to imagine someone having to die like that. We all have this imagine of dying in a hospital bed or in hospice, taking our last few breaths with family around, but this is not always the case with death. Cause of death is usually determined later by the medical examiner, but as officers we have to estimate an "apparent cause of death" during our investigation. Depending on the age of the victim, their previous known health conditions, and other factors, we essentially have to rule out suspicious circumstances or suicide and accidental injury, all which would require more investigation. Everything else falls into the category of "natural causes." I ask you, however, are there any natural ways to die? Is a heart attack or aneurism at just forty years old natural? The answer to this, to me anyway, is no. I have a very hard time dealing with people who suddenly die who are not very old and sickly.

I can sometimes justify things such as heart attacks by circumstances, such as the obesity of the person. I might tell myself, OK, this person died because they did not take care of themselves; they essentially sealed their own fate. This is not always the case though.

One time, I had responded to a hotel within town for a well-being check on a guy who was traveling with a business group who did not show up for the noontime meeting. Upon entering the hotel room, I located him dead on the floor in his workout clothes next to his bed. The individual was very fit and had apparently exercised earlier in the morning. His body was still relatively warm but was cooling, which indicated his time of death sometime in the morning. The medical examiner showed up because of this man's young age and the circumstances. After speaking with his business partners, they advised us they all flew in last night and had dinner. They advised they all went to their rooms and were going to meet for lunch the next day. I'll never forget the medical examiner rolling this guy over and nonchalantly saying, "He probably got a blood clot from the plane flight." This never sat well with me.

Wait—what? That can happen? I thought.

I am not OK with this. People are supposed to die for a valid reason, such as old age and being chronically ill; they just don't randomly die, especially young people.

This also affected me personally, as my father is a businessman who frequently travels. How in that moment do you not think of your own family in that situation? This could be my father on one of his business trips. This someone's husband and father, and now he isn't answering his cell phone. There is nothing worse than being on a death call and seeing the deceased person's cell phone ringing with "Mom" (or someone else's name that might be a spouse) calling continuously.

My wife doesn't fully understand that this is why I get so upset when she doesn't answer her phone. I am not just thinking, *You're busy or in the shower*—my mind goes to the worst place. This is what PTSD does. Every time I have to travel by plane, I see the image of this poor guy lying on the hotel room floor with his workout clothes and me feeling his back for temperature. After this incident, I now worry that while sitting on a plane, I could be getting a clot and I nervously try to wiggle my legs and feet to keep moving. Usually going to bed the night after traveling, I worry that my wife or I may develop get a clot while sleeping or sometime expectantly during the next day.

These are not only fears from the enemy but they are symptoms of PTSD. PTSD is not just from combat; it is from repeated exposure to images and circumstances that can affect you mentally and physically.

Finding people dead in hotel rooms is not uncommon. I dislike one hotel chain in particular because I responded to a few sudden deaths there. I can't help but wonder when staying in a hotel if someone ever died in the room I am staying in. These are disturbing thoughts that the average person never thinks about. This brings us back to what I have said earlier about exposure. The world first responders live in exposes them to circumstances that are rare to the average person. An average person may not ever be exposed to these types of incidents; therefore, they assume these events never happen or they just don't ever think about them.

"Accidents happen." This is a popular phrase we hear often, and someone like me can attest to this. This is why when I see a family member doing something I think is unsafe, I can't help but cringe and have to say something. The response I usually get, though, is that I am overly paranoid and a worrywart. What they don't understand is that I have seen these things happen to happen, and they do happen.

I responded to the person who fell off the ladder cleaning gutters and died, the person who cut his hand with the table saw, and the guy who shot his hand while cleaning his gun. No one ever thinks tragedy will strike—well, except for someone like me. Tragedy looms over my existence as a constant fear, no doubt brought on by the enemy and the environment I've been exposed to. I have seen tragedy strike repeatedly and cannot help but wonder when it will strike me.

* * * * *

One of the greatest issues I've struggled with on these types of calls has to do with the grieving family members. I cannot distance myself from them and separate my emotions. Even though these people are strangers, they are human and their grief is very real, and seeing people like this over and over can take a serious toll on your mind.

Ever had to tell someone that a loved one has died? Delivering this kind of news is one of the worst things you can do. Police officers are often called upon to deliver death notifications to family members when someone dies. There is no easy way to do this, and I have found that you just have to come out and say it as quickly as possible so they can process it. No one ever thinks about the toll this takes on us to constantly have to bear these burdens, which—if you're exposed to them repeatedly—can send you into the darkness which is depression, anxiety, and PTSD.

I am haunted not only by the images of the dead but of the living who are grieving. I can hear the screaming and wailing of mourning family members. I have had to physically restrain grieving family from getting to their loved one until the scene had been processed. I have been screamed and cussed at by family for not saving their loved one and accused of lying about their death or simply not doing enough to save them. I do not blame these people one bit; I would be just as hysterical. Death causes so many feelings of sadness and anger, and I have to stand there and take the brunt of it while I try to still do my job and collect all the necessary information I need for the police report. This is an awful and very awkward feeling trying to probe the victim's family for information while also trying not to upset them or seem insensitive.

Later on in my career, I began to have a very difficult time on these calls and a few times actually brought myself to tears when speaking to the family, expressing my sympathy. The reality of it is, I truly am sympathetic and I feel just terrible for them and what I have to do to complete my report. On one of my very last sudden death calls, a religious woman suffering from the final stages of cancer lost her husband suddenly to a heart attack. While on the call, she was crying next to him sitting on the floor. I felt the sudden need to kneel down next to her. Holding both of her hands, I said to her with tears in my eyes, "Look at me, he's not here. The body is imperfect, it is only a vessel." I expressed to her how truly sorry I was with a tear rolling down my cheek. In this moment her pain became my pain, and it was very real.

> *For we know that when this earthly tent we live in is taken down (that is, when we die and leave this earthly body), we have a house in heaven, an eternal body made for us by God himself and not by human hands.*
> 2 CORINTHIANS 5:1

A few years ago is when I started to notice my problem with viewing the deceased. A young man in his early twenties was found by his friend, dead inside his car in a garage. The furnace in the garage had been running, and the carbon monoxide detector was on the floor of the garage with the batteries taken out next to it. Every sign here in my investigation, including the text message argument with his girlfriend during the moments prior, made this appear like a suicide. I don't know exactly why—maybe it was his age, or maybe I just had enough but I could not look at him lying there dead in the car. To make matters worse, almost every family member and person in the town who ever knew him showed up at the house while he was still in the garage. I kid you not, there was anywhere from twenty to twenty-five people on the front lawn freaking out. His mother and sister arrived and were in hysterics, and I needed to try to collect information to figure out if this was indeed a suicide or an accident. Turns out, I never really could say exactly. This young man had come home that night severely intoxicated and had been fighting with his girlfriend over text about his drinking habits.

According to his family, he had everything going for him and had no signs of depression. I got the gist that the family did not like the girlfriend too much, but they said their son was not the type to kill himself over a girlfriend; he would have just shrugged it off and moved on to the next. It was possible that he went out to vent, sitting in his car in the garage while he drank, then removed the carbon monoxide alarm because it was irritating him, but his text messages to girlfriend ("I love you goodbye") seemed to indicate something else.

Either way, this was very tragic, and he was too young to die. This call was a turning point for me, and from here on out, I had a really hard time looking at deceased people. I just cannot shake specific images from my mind, like the image of a person being loaded and zipped into a heavy-duty crinkly blue plastic sterile-looking body bag. It's almost as if the body is treated like medical waste at this point. While I know this is not true, perhaps there can be a more sensitive way of removing the body from the scene. When we see dead people in a funeral home, they are adorned by flowers and a velvet-lined casket. While this is still very morbid, it is much better than that cold, hard blue bag of death they zip you in to wheel you out.

This is a very hard image for me to rid myself of, and it's difficult not to imagine myself—or even worse, my children, wife, or anyone in my family—lifeless and cold being placed in the same uncomfortable bag then in the back of a vehicle. I could cry thinking about how terrible death presents itself in this way: a person reduced to medical waste in a plastic zippered bag. I don't know, maybe if it were less sterile and maybe if it were open near the head, I would be better with it, but I just have a very difficult time with this to the point it makes me feel ill.

Going back to the call ...

One of our crime scene specialists showed up to process the scene, which helped me because I was able to avoid looking at the body. I believe God was trying to protect me going forward, saying, Don't look anymore. He knew I had reached my limit and what was bothering me, but so does the enemy. God, however, will prevail and he has removed me from this line of work for what I feel is for good.

I have always feared seeing the death of a child, and since having children, I know I would not be able to handle it mentally. Unfortunately, as a police officer I cannot control where I am sent and what I might see, so I have to come to the realization, this is no longer my place. I believe God has recently confirmed this for me one morning while I was fighting a morning bout of anxiety.

Lying in bed that morning the thought popped into my head:

I am getting you out of there. I didn't think this up myself, and my original intention was to return to work, but at that moment I did not hear the voice of God but rather felt it. This was really a turning point for me, as I never really intended of leaving police work when this originally all happened. During moments of uncertainty, I have to keep reminding myself of the message that morning and remember that through these trials God has a plan and he is in control.

* * * * *

Responding to calls with deceased people usually includes strong sensory experiences, and I think that is why they lend themselves to a large part of PTSD. The different sights, smells, sounds, and tactile experiences on these calls tend to burn into our minds. I mentioned the families screaming and wailing, but there is also the image of CPR and resuscitation attempts that leave a lasting impression. I have always hated the sight of CPR. Pumping on the chest of a lifeless body while the body shakes about while the family desperately watches is horrific. Medical items are scattered about on the floor; the victim is often intubated with a tube down their throat. The machine they sometimes use to perform CPR that continuously pumps the chest is even more horrific to watch on top of all of this.

After the rescue does everything in their power, they reach a point where they pronounce the person deceased, and then they grab their equipment and leave. Now you, the police officer, are stuck there with a dead person, with an intubation tube sticking out of their mouth and all plastic medical waste scattered about the floor. Now comes the part of dealing with the family.

In some cases, you are unlucky enough to arrive before the

rescue and have to start CPR yourself. I don't know if you have ever performed CPR on a real person, but it is much different than on a dummy, listening to the rhythm of the Bee Gee's "Staying Alive." CPR training would be more realistic if you had family screaming, "Papa, get up!" at their loved one you while you pump away, cracking their ribs.

When I performed CPR on one such occasion, the person's ribs were broken, and there was no feedback whatsoever. The person's chest was like jelly, and I could not even feel where the breast bone was at that point as I tried to continue to push. The thought of it still makes me gag and is much different than the metallic audible feedback of doing it on a CPR dummy.

I told my psychiatrist that I associate CPR with death, as I have never seen a person revived by it. Usually when I hear "CPR in progress" that means the person is already dead and they're just making a last-ditch attempt to save them. Put simply, I hate the image of CPR being performed in real life and associate trauma and tragedy with it.

* * * * *

Another issue that bothers me with death calls is the environment and circumstances that people often die in. It's not uncommon to have people die on the toilet, for example. I once had a woman die while cleaning her floor with a mop. Her friend had gone to check on her and found her fallen and wedged partially standing into the corner of the kitchen wall. As soon as I arrived, it appeared as if she had just recently fainted or passed out, as she was kind of still standing and clutching the mop and bucket. I immediately went to grab her and lower her to the floor; however, when I pulled on her arms, they pulled back and were stiff as stone. I immediately let go with a shriek of disgust and surprise, realizing rigor had set in—a sign she had, in fact, been long dead. In circumstances like this, there isn't much you can do at this point but wait for the crime scene specialist. There is no point in calling in a rescue if the person displays "signs inconsistent with life." Having rigor mortis is one of these. Clear suicides and fatal car accidents mainly consist of the other types of signs.

I responded to a 911 call one time in which the caller was crying and screaming hysterically that the dispatcher could not make out what they were saying. When I arrived, I went into the kitchen and found a man wailing hysterically on the floor. I tried to talk to him, but he was so hysterical I don't even think he knew I was there. I noticed a light coming from the door to the basement behind me, and I cautiously made my way down. To my horror, I found a woman in a bathrobe hanging from the basement ceiling. She had been hanging so long that the rope and her neck had begun to stretch to the point that her feet were pretty much almost flat on the ground. Strangely, my first instinct was to cut her down, but then I stopped myself once I realized she was dead.

* * * * *

These are the images and circumstances that are hard to process as well. Death is not natural; suicide is even more so not natural. God never intended for us to take our own lives. Suicide is truly the work and victory of the enemy. It brings suffering to many and is often gory and horrific by nature. Suicide by pills and overdose is probably the most common form we see, but suicide by firearm is probably the second most common.

I responded one night to a father who shot himself in the head with a snub-nose .38 caliber on the front porch with his wife and kids home. It was wintertime, and he had been arguing with his family. During the argument, he retrieved his gun from the safe and began to wave it around, threatening to shoot himself. Apparently, according to the family, we learned this was something he did rather often, so they did not take him seriously anymore. Well, that night, he saw it through and walked out the front door onto their front porch and shot a round right into his head.

We found him lying facedown on the stairs of the porch with his feet on the stoop and his head at the bottom of the stairs. Because it was so cold, by the time the crime scene specialist got there, the pool of blood around his head was starting to congeal and the crime scene tech was picking it up with a pen like a piece of paper.

The worst part of that call was that he did it in front of the kids. These kids were little (probably no more than eleven years old). We had to hold a sheet up in front of the body. That way we could walk the kids out by the garage so they couldn't see him. I had to drive these kids to their grandmother's house from there. We later had a lot of dealings with both of them, as they were very troubled when they got older.

* * * * *

As I finished writing this chapter, I became overwhelmed with anxiety. My heart pounded and my mind began to race. Over the next two days I had some rough periods. I had a fear that I might have this reaction. Strangely enough, while writing I did not have as severe as a reaction, but hours later I paid the toll.

I apologize for anyone that experienced any discomfort reading any of this. I hope you will never experience this kind of trauma in your lifetime and will appreciate what first responders have to do day in and day out. This is not an easy job, and it is not for everyone. Even I have reached my limit after twelve years' exposure to trauma. I am told PTSD is cumulative, meaning that it builds upon itself from multiple incidents, and that's what I'm currently experiencing. Death is not something we should be exposed to continually. The human mind and body can only handle so much.

CHAPTER 12

THE BEGINNING SIGNS: PHYSICAL MANIFESTATIONS <u>OF</u> FEAR

"Don't be afraid, for I am with you. Do not be discouraged, for I am your God. I will strengthen you and help you, I will hold you up with my victorious hand."
Isaiah 41:10

In early 2018, I developed acid reflux that was so severe I had trouble drinking water, let alone eating even the blandest of foods. I saw doctors and specialists, then went on a proton pump inhibitor, but no matter what I did, I could not find relief. I ended up having my dosage slowly increased until I reached the highest possible dosage.

After several months, I reached a point of survivability, but I would still get bad flare-ups. I had an endoscopy done, which really did not reveal anything. My gastroenterologist seemed perplexed, as I did not fit the typical mold for acid reflux. I don't drink or smoke, and I'm not overweight. She considered other ailments that mimic reflux disorder, but ultimately we never really found out what caused it.

Eventually, after almost a year on medication, I felt normal again and could pretty much eat and drink whatever I wanted.

Now I'm on a much lower dose and pretty much symptom-free, thank God. The beginning of 2019, however, brought other medical issues for me, and they seemed to be happening one after another.

First, I started having issues with my left eye, which felt extremely sensitive to light, and at times my vision was blurry. I wear contacts daily and assumed the problem would resolve itself, but it continued for a little over a month. So I saw my primary doctor about my vision, as well as an optometrist. My primary care doctor chalked it up to stress or perhaps Lyme disease. My optometrist thought it may have been mainly neurological, as everything appeared healthy in the examination, and also stated stress and Lyme as a possibility.

After this began to subside, I was sitting in my patrol car one day and began to have a burning sensation on the top of my right foot. I assumed, at the time, that my duty belt pressing on my spine was responsible. And I had some soreness in my right upper thigh that would occasionally irritate me. Doing the rational thing, I visited my chiropractor, who believed the issue could have been sciatic related, which is exactly what I believed as well.

As this continued, I began to notice my left leg was now experiencing burning and numbness, as well as my left hand on and off. I have to admit, I was starting to get extremely paranoid, considering my recent eye issues—and now the numbness—that the two were somehow related to a more serious underlying condition. As I was driving into work one day, this only got worse in both of my legs, starting with a cold burning sensation traveling up both legs. I began to get nervous and called out of work and went straight to the chiropractor. Perplexed, the chiropractor did not understand what was causing such "inflammation." He sent me for some X-rays, which came out negative. I continued to see him and do exercises and stretching at home.

Around this same time frame, I was involved in a foot pursuit. I mentioned this earlier in the book, and I think it was just another nail in the coffin. This pursuit happened first thing in the morning at the start of my shift, and it was really a huge jump start for the day.

Another month went by, and I went on a call with a town regular we always dealt with. This lady had a previous brain injury and was mostly just a drunk and harmless. I had been dealing with her since day one on the job. She loved police attention and would often call us, asking to go to the hospital and saying she wanted to kill herself, and would be waiting for us with her bags ready when we got there. This time her behavior was different; she didn't seem herself and appeared to be crying and deeply disturbed. She ran into her bedroom, and another officer and I tried to talk her into going to the hospital. Suddenly, out of nowhere she lunged for a pair of scissors and lifted them high to strike. Caught off guard, the other officer and I grabbed her by both arms, scissors still in hand. This was an awakening moment for me. I had let my guard down and become complacent with her. She, I, or my partner could have been hurt. This somehow affected me.

A few weeks later, I responded for an unresponsive male in a restaurant bathroom. The guy was one of the cooks, and he was found by another staff member unresponsive in the bathroom. It had really only been an hour since the other guy last had contact with him, and the victim had been complaining of stomach pain. The rescue arrived first and began CPR, but it was too late. They worked him for the required thirty minutes per the state protocol and then pronounced him dead on scene. I tried not to look, knowing my issues now with dead people, but I had to go into the bathroom to retrieve his cellphone. I couldn't help but notice him lying on the floor of the bathroom, his shirt ripped open by rescue and a medical intubation tube still sticking out of his mouth. The fire department suspected he had a heart attack due to his stomach complaints, which apparently are related. At that point, I couldn't help but think if I had a stomachache and the runs, I could be victim of a heart attack soon.

In the weeks that followed, I started getting a new problem. Upon arriving at work one day, I got out of my personal car and began walking to the station. I suddenly was stopped dead in my tracks by a stabbing pain through my left eye into the left temple of my head. I have never felt anything like this before. The pain subsided moments later, but I was now frightened.

I once responded to a man who dropped in the middle of the aisle of a grocery store that was seen clutching his head seconds before he collapsed. Concerned this was serious, I tried to go about my day, but I continued to have pain on and off around my left temple. I took migraine medicine, but this persisted for about two weeks and always seemed to get worse when I was heading into work in the morning in the parking lot of the police station.

I will be honest and say that at this point, as I was thinking about all of the issues that had been bothering me over the last couple of months, I was getting concerned something serious wa s going on. Why is all this stuff happening?

* * * * *

The following week, I was going into work, and as I'm getting changed in the locker room I start to panic.

My heart starts rapidly pounding, and my vision is suddenly

narrowing. I'm trying to focus on getting dressed. My peripheral vision is fading and blurry. My chest is feeling tight. With each breath is sharp pain, which travels up my chest into my neck. I feel like the world is closing in, and this sudden weight and pressure building and weighing down on me. I'm fighting the feeling of paranoia in my mind of being suddenly confined and somehow dizzy at the same time. I try to ignore the feeling as I'm getting dressed, and the normal locker room banter from the other guys is the room just muffled and overshadowed by the sound and feeling of my pounding heart.

I sit down in my usual spot in roll call, and while the sergeant was speaking, I have this urge to just scream from inside me, as I'm so uncomfortable. Normally after the sergeant finishes his brief, we usually sit around and talk for a few minutes before we have to drag ourselves up to get ready and load our cars for the day.

I ask the sergeant if he's done and then quickly run outside, trying to go about my day and load my cruiser, hoping the feeling will just subside. I begin driving down the road, but the feeling is building inside me. I'm trying to put it aside, but it is rapidly overcoming me. I pull into an empty parking lot behind a building and immediately start crying and gasping for air. Any radio transmission at this point is a blur—I'm focusing on slowing my heart rate and being able to breathe. I feel a mixture of fear and confusion. I'm just so afraid. I've lost all control of my mind and my body, and I'm frightened.

I look up at the sky toward God and yell, "WHAT'S WRONG WITH ME?"

I call my wife and she tells me, "You need to come home."

I drive back to the station and collect myself enough to go up to the desk supervisor. I tell him, "I'm not sure what's going on, but I feel like my body is literally falling apart and I just need to go home." He sends me home, and as I leave his office, I tell him, "I'll be in tomorrow."

I head down into the locker room, get undressed, then just sit there on one of the chairs, unable to really move and not ready to drive away yet unsure what was happening to me. Finally, I pull myself up to leave and get in my car.

That describes what happened the last time I stepped foot in that building.

After leaving the station, I drive to an empty lot and start to call people to talk to for help: one of my other work friends and the department chaplain. I sit there and talk to both of them before driving home.

The next seventy-two hours were hell. I had never felt so uncomfortable in my own skin. If I could have jumped out of my skin, I would have. I walked around the house pacing, unable to sit, unable to calm down. I started shaking at night in bed and throughout the next couple of days. I went to the emergency room with my wife and told them everything that has been happening over the last few months. I told them I was a police officer and I had developed this unhealthy fear of dying and of an underlying illness because of all the things I had seen people die from.

The ER doctor was an extremely nice woman, and she genuinely seemed very concerned and compassionate. Sitting there explaining everything to her, I am crying and shaking and saying how guilty I feel for putting my wife through this. She tells me she is going to run a bunch of blood work and do a head scan to be on the safe side and rule out anything serious. She gives me a lorazepam to calm down, and I proceed with all the tests. The tests eventually come back negative, and she tells me to speak to my primary doctor about anxiety.

A day later, I go to my primary care doctor, and I tell the physician assistant about everything I have been experiencing and the fears I have developed as a police officer. She prescribes me an antianxiety medication for which you gradually have to increase the dosage over the next few weeks.

My heart pounds in my chest. The terror of death assaults me. Fear and trembling overwhelm me, and I can't stop shaking.
PSALM 55:4-5

Does this sound familiar? I have a fear of death. I have come to acknowledge this. I fear my death and that of my loved ones. This fear has manifested in paranoia and physical symptoms. I have seen so many people die from sudden causes. I fear most what I cannot predict or control. The Bible, however, tells us:

Do not be anxious about anything, but in every situation, by prayer and petition, with thanksgiving, present your requests to God. And the peace of the God, which transcends all understanding, will guard your hearts and your minds in Christ Jesus.
PHILIPPIANS 4:6-7 NIV

A few days later, I heard this passage on a Christian radio station while in the car with my wife. This was one of God's many first attempts to knock at my door. The days after leaving work were horrendous, and I was descending very rapidly into darkness. I became barely functional and would stay in bed in the morning and just rock, unable to move or get up.

During this period, I was uncomfortable, confused, afraid, and unable to even leave the house.

* * * * *

One day my wife convinced me to go out with the kids to get some ice cream. While sitting in the ice cream store, I immediately began to panic and requested we leave. It was during the very beginning that I began to look for God for help. I prayed very often for help but felt very alone.

At times, I would have mental conversations in my head with God while lying in bed, but most of this consisted of my own thoughts. One morning, however, while doing this and feeling alone, I felt the words, I'm here—nothing more and nothing less but just enough. At the time, it wasn't exactly the immediate miracle I was waiting for, but it was something and it was not prompted by my own thoughts.

During the beginning of all this, I had hoped to be rid of my anxiety and fear of death and simply return to work. What I did not understand was if my bill of health from all the tests from the ER were clean, then why hadn't I snapped out of it? Instead I felt as if I was getting much worse. I knew there was nothing medically wrong; in fact, all of the headaches and numbness were gone, now replaced by terrible unrelenting anxiety.

I had taken some time out of work on vacation, but as the end of it was approaching, I knew I was not ready to go back. I had been on the antianxiety medication for two weeks and was able to leave the house at least, but I was still battling periods of severe anxiety, especially at night through the morning.

During that time, my wife and I went out for a weekend alone while my mother watched the kids. We ended up meeting a very strange, flamboyant man and his wife, who originated from Ghana, while sitting by the hotel pool. This guy happened to be sitting next to us and was throwing his money around like it was nothing. He had gold rings on every finger and tried to strike up a conversation with me.

"You having a good time, my friend?" he asks me.

Listening to music, I remove my headphones. "Yeah."

"You don't look very relaxed," he says. "Come, let me buy you and your wife a drink, anything you want. Relax."

"Oh, no thanks. I'm on medication, I can't drink."

Persistent, he asked me what kind of medication I was on, and that opened up the door for the conversation as I began telling him my story.

What he says next strikes me as odd, as I was not expecting this from him. "Listen, my friend," he says. "God is telling me to tell you this: You need to tell your boss at work."

At this point, I never considered having to notify work, because I thought the anxiety was just going to go away by the time the leave I took was up. As the days got closer to the end of my time off, however, I realized he was right. I had not gotten better, and the thought of just returning to that job was giving me severe anxiety.

I decided to call someone on the peer support team and tell them what was happening. The officer told me, "Sounds like you have PTSD" and asked if I would be willing to talk to a clinician. I agreed, and I began speaking to her on a weekly basis.

I was eventually diagnosed with PTSD related to work as a police officer. I will say this about psychotherapy: Once you start opening up the can of worms, all the other issues come out. I realized that my PTSD was not just from fear of dying but all of the images associated it with it that I have seen and all of the stress my body had been through from constantly going into that primal "fight or flight" mode on a daily basis.

I learned that many of the physical ailments I was experiencing were something called somatic symptoms, and it was my body's way of manifesting the stress. The best way it was described to me was that my cup was full and had now overflowed. Unfortunately, while psychotherapy is good, it also involved reliving many of the very issues that caused my PTSD and rediscovering incidents and traumas I'd been exposed to in my twelve years in law enforcement. In the months that ensued, battling PTSD brought a myriad of new and varying symptoms through my battle with this darkness, but at the same time, it also forced me to seek out God even more.

CHAPTER 13

FAITH IN THE FIRE: FINDING LIGHT IN DARKNESS

These trials will show you that your faith is genuine.
It is being tested as fire tests and purifies gold.
1 PETER 1:7

In the beginning after my diagnosis, my symptoms were very severe and persistent. Each day brought more anxiety and more symptoms. I began to experience things that gave me even more cause for alarm. I noticed that I was at times very irritable. This still happens on occasion but seems less frequent. I noticed I am more irritable when things are weighing on my mind. If there are too many issues going on at the same time, I feel overwhelmed and my stress turns into aggression.

During the beginning of this, my wife continued to work while I had to stay home watching the kids. At first, I did not feel comfortable by myself with them. Not that I would ever hurt them or myself, but I did not want to get into a state of panic or anger around them. Kids in general can push buttons and make you irritable, but imagine already being in a high state of irritability.

When I met with my clinician, I would tell her that I was experiencing different feelings that sometimes scared me. I felt like I was at times not in control of my own emotions and my mind. I was also adjusting to the anti-anxiety medication and would

160

frequently notice a change and worsening in symptoms anytime I initially had to up my dosage.

Not feeling very comfortable with my mental state, I would take the kids and drive to my in-laws' house for the day, just so I was not alone. This also helped me get my mind out of my own head, as conversing with others can be a distraction. I will tell you that fear, worry, and guilt can often accompany PTSD. At times, I felt I was burdening my family and could be putting a serious financial strain on us, leading to a future of uncertainty. I felt so guilty around my wife and my children that I was not the strong father I had been.

My kids are both very small and really don't understand what's going on, but my oldest one (who is four at the time of writing this) began to pick up on some of my conversations and detected that Daddy was sick. When I would look at my children, I felt like I had failed them. I was a police officer, this was my job, this was how I paid the bills and did my part to support the family, and now I was not doing that. Instead, I felt very broken as a person, as a husband, and as a father. I felt very alone and at times had some strange intrusive thoughts that were not thoughts of my own.

* * * * *

One day while watching my kids, I was sitting on the sofa with my daughter, who was not doing anything wrong but just sitting there. One of her things she does for comfort is she likes to rub your earlobes. Sometimes, when I feel certain emotions and feelings set in, I get very closed off and almost irked by them crawling on me or touching me. When I get like this, I want them off me, not touching me, and I feel almost a primal sense of defensiveness, even though these are my children, whom I love more than anything in the world.

That day I felt a horrible feeling coming over me. I felt such a defensive anger and an evil. I can tell you these were not thoughts of my own, and they were frightening me more than anything in my life.

The only way I can explain it was pure evil. I knew these thoughts and feelings were from the enemy and he was waging war on me by trying to put thoughts and images in my head. I could not help but wonder why I was so susceptible for attack. It was in this very moment I knew evil was genuinely real and a strong force to be reckoned with. The enemy was launching an unrelenting full-frontal attack. This feeling weighed heavily on me for the next day, it was such a dark, overbearing feeling.

The next day while searching the internet, I came across a Twitter post from September, 17, 2018 by Christian author and psychologist Dr. Henry Cloud that affirmed this: "Just because a thought comes into your head doesn't mean you have to grab it. Most of the negative or fearful ones are just noise. Leave them alone. They will fall on their own weight if you don't dance with them or fuel them."[4]

Talk about timing, I read this, and it immediately affirmed what I was thinking. Not only that, but this was an old Twitter post, and God showed me that he operates outside of time when he made me find that post. I was dwelling on the origin of this thought, as it was very concerning to me, but then I realized the enemy wanted me to dwell on the thoughts and question their origin. I had to let the thoughts drop and disappear.

---

4. Dr. Henry Cloud, Twitter, September 17, 2018, https://twitter.com/DrHenryCloud/status/1041848655156609025.

You are just noise! You have no power over me! Our almighty God is greater than you! Run and cower in the name of Jesus!

While those thoughts have never resurfaced, I still get moments of agitation where the noise of my children—either yelling, singing, screaming, or banging and dropping toys—creates a primal reaction in me. When I get like this, I get extremely freaked about the touching or pulling at me and just want to be alone, but they don't understand this. I feel awful when I'm like this. My kids don't understand, and I feel bad about my short temper and aversion to their clinginess and touching. What is interesting about this is that I don't always feel this way, and like everything else with PTSD, it comes and goes in intensity.

* * * * *

During my journey with PTSD, I had been experiencing very odd feelings and almost felt like I was in a psychosis, like an altered state of reality, almost delusional. I began to get intrusive thoughts that I knew were not right. As police officers we would often deal with the mentally ill, and paranoid schizophrenia is a common thing we see. This is a terrible illness, and I would argue one caused by the enemy himself to make you think and believe strange things. These people often think they are being controlled by some outside force, and their mind was being probed by radio waves from the TV set or the government.

Strangely enough I began to have feelings in my head myself that something was there, taking up space, like an insect that I was desperately trying to rip out like in a sci-fi movie. I had this feeling of pressure like something was there on the left side of my head, which was driving me literally insane.

I began to question every noise around me, as I was in tune to every ambient noise that normally I would never pay attention to. I heard humming and would search the house, only to find it was coming from the laptop's internal fan in the other room. I would desperately try to validate that what I was hearing was real and I was not going crazy.

This feeling did not just occur with hearing but my other senses as well. One day while walking on the floor, I felt as though I stepped in something wet on the bottom of my foot but could not locate the water or the source on the floor. I do believe it was only a very tiny bit of waterdrops from my child's bottle, but when I had stepped in it and could not see it on the floor, I began to question the sensation I was feeling and if it was real.

I met with my clinician and was initially afraid to tell her my experiences because I did not want to accept I might be going crazy. To my relief, she verified what I was going through was typical for PTSD and that the "switch" in my brain that rationalizes my senses and thoughts was temporarily off and out of synch.

While this is mostly of medical nature, I attribute this also to the enemy's doing.

Be alert and of sober mind. Your enemy the devil prowls around like a roaring lion looking for someone to devour.

1 PETER 5:8 NIV

For our struggle is not against flesh and blood, but against the rulers, against the authorities, against the powers of this dark world and against the spiritual forces of evil in the heavenly realms.

EPHESIANS 6:12 NIV

It was during this period that I knew I was under severe attack. I had also recently begun praying daily and seeking out God more than ever. In this process, I realized that my past sins were holding me back, and I started to feel great guilt about this. I felt that God was revealing my weakness to me that was allowing the enemy in.

Do not conform to the pattern of this world, but be transformed by the renewing of your mind. Then you will be able to test and approve what God's will is— his good, pleasing and perfect will.

ROMANS 12:2 NIV

Sitting there alone one day, I suddenly felt so convicted with guilt. I felt disgusted and began to cry, telling God I was ashamed and I wanted to be a better husband and a father going forward. I stood up with my eyes closed, sobbing, and imagined myself being embraced by Jesus

I believe from that moment on is when I started on the right path. I began to turn to the Bible and pray for freedom from sin and temptation, and I am glad to say that I am in so much of a better place now. I am still on a journey, but I confessed my struggles to the Lord, and he has helped me overcome it and for the most part I now have control over it. I also felt some relief after that when it came to the fear of my own death.

I sought the Lord, and he answered me; he delivered me from all my fears.

PSALM 34:4 NIV

As I started reading the Bible, I began in Psalms, reading the writings of David then turned to Paul's letters in the New Testament. These letters are great instructions for Christians and mostly applicable to today as well. Moving on to the Gospels, I read the stories of Jesus in a different light than what I was familiar with as a child. I am still nowhere near scratching the surface of the Bible, but I cannot believe the amount of context in it that is so applicable to my own struggles. The Bible also amazingly references past scriptures and teaching, and everything that is separated by so much time from the Old Testament is somehow prophesied and connected in the New Testament. It's all really amazing that this book continues to withstand the evil world we live in.

If you are a new Christian, a prospective Christian, or current one and you haven't read God's Word, then you have to explore it yourself. Trust me, seek out the Word and just read—it almost reads itself to you. Nothing teaches about God, creation, evil, and human struggle like the Bible does.

Your word is a lamp for my feet, a light on my path.
PSALM 119:105 NIV

My journey to salvation has not been an easy one, and it has not been without hurdles. At times, I still tend to question God and his existence. I have never done this before in my life more than I have done in the past couple of months. I can't help but feel if I am coming to God more, longing for relationship and wisdom, then why is it that I'm doubting now more than ever. I just believed with blind faith as a child growing up, and now I read the Scriptures and meditate, but I find myself plagued by doubt. I have been told that when you try to get closer to God, this is when the enemy kicks things into overdrive. He fears he is losing you to God, and he will do everything in his power to pull you back.

One day while sleeping, I woke suddenly with a thought in my head that I have never thought of before. If there is a God, where did he come from? Who created him? How could he just exist? How could that be possible? You are being good for nothing, depriving yourself pleasure for no reason.

This is when I became skeptical of this thought and saw the agenda behind it. The enemy just wants me to go back to my own ways.

I had never ever, ever questioned God's existence before this, even when I was sinner. Why now when I was trying so hard to come to God and the light was I beginning to doubt? Then the following scripture popped up on my daily devotional on my phone: "But I fear that somehow your pure and undivided devotion to Christ will be corrupted, just as Eve was deceived by the cunning ways of the serpent" (2 Corinthians 11:3).

I have to give God credit that he is fighting back and continuing to send me Scripture, but I confess I still struggle at times.

* * * * *

Recently I started having questions about the creation timeline and evolution as relates to Scripture. While it was good that I was reading and considering the Word, perhaps I was overanalyzing things. I often make the mistake of looking for answers on the internet, but I decided to ask God instead. I asked for forgiveness for questioning him, but maybe he could help me understand.

The following day I felt like God led me to come across a couple of readings from various different Christian apologists with views on how God is outside of what we know of as humans who are limited by time and space. This helped me understand when the Bible says God has no beginning or end.

"I am the Alpha and the Omega, the First and the Last, the Beginning and the End" (Revelation 22:13).

God does not play by the rules of human physics; he isn't human. He operates outside the realm we live in. As humans we tend to want to put things into a three-dimensional perspective that we can see, touch, and understand. I wanted to understand how something or someone could come from nothing. The fact is, God is not something or someone limited by our ways of comprehension. We are bound by our understanding of science and our physical world.

Just recently, an article caught my attention in which a prominent modern-day scholar made the claim that "there is no God." I then wondered about all these prominent intelligent "scholars" out there who place physics and science before God, then the word came to me: pride. I felt as though God was saying, These people are too prideful with their own intellect that they fail to acknowledge me. Doing so will hurt their ego, as they simply lack humility.

Science has created arrogance. The King James Version of 1 Timothy 6:20 puts it best—we are to avoid "vain babblings, and oppositions of science."

> As the Scriptures say, "I will destroy the wisdom of the wise and discard the intelligence of the intelligent." So where does this leave the philosophers, the scholars, and the world's brilliant debaters? God has made the wisdom of this world look foolish.

1 CORINTHIANS 1:19-20

Sitting in bed praying the other night, I asked God again for divine wisdom, like he granted King Solomon, to discern what I was reading in the Bible, my own thoughts, and other things I may see and hear that may dispute God. Then I felt as though I suddenly realized God was showing me that I already had the wisdom and was coming to the answers. I also felt as though God was asking me, Do you feel me?

And I have to say, Yes, I do. I can't understand with my own mind how I was able to break away from certain sins, I can't understand with my own mind how I was able to pull myself out of the darkness that was trying to swallow me whole at the very start of this. While I am still struggling with PTSD and moments of sadness, I realize it is an ongoing battle.

* * * * *

One night, I had a very interesting dream.

I am trapped in a building which seems like a high school, and it is engulfed in fire. As I am trying to escape the heat, and smoke all around me, the doors are blocked and won't open. Something I could not identify among the flames was across from me. I cannot see what it is, but it is scaring me. I remember I have the power in Jesus' name and begin to cast demons away in his name. The flames immediately scatter like the demons, who bow in fear, recognizing Jesus as the Son of God in the Gospels. I am not only able to move aside flames, but I am also able to break up the blockages and cast open the doors, for my escape. The feeling is so gratifying and amazing.

Usually in dreams, nothing works like you want it to. I often would have the dream of defending myself with a gun that shot slow or useless bullets. In this dream, however, I am stunned by the immediate power I have as I make my way out of the building. Suddenly, once outside the building and safe, I feel the need to go back in and help others, and I do just that, dragging out an injured person caught in the building. Maybe this is God's way of showing me that I have the power to be strong in Christ and am going to help others. Maybe this whole circumstance I am in right now is meant to bring me closer to God.

I cannot say that all my dreams have been positive. I have had several dreams lately where I have physically lashed out in bed after being attacked in my dreams by unknown creatures unrelentingly pursuing me, only to have my wife waking me up with her hand blocking me in a defensive position. Frequently I have dreams where I am back on a police call and my heart may pound and I might start sweating. I recently had a dream that I was at work, and I suddenly woke up while lunging for a suspect only to realize I'm in bed at home.

PTSD is a strange beast. Even though my mind is in a much better place now, my body still reacts to certain situations. I have found, for example, that running up a flight of stairs, even in my own home, mimics the response of "fight or flight" in me, almost as if I am preparing to go into a house, apartment, or dangerous situation on a call. When I reach the top landing of my second floor, my heart begins to pound and a feeling of anxiety overcomes me. I get this same feeling every time I am about to leave the house for the day. Isn't it interesting how my body is responding to a certain stimulus that brings my mind back to circumstances at work? I told my clinician I don't feel as though I am consciously thinking or worried about anything when this comes on, but instead it's my body and mind's subconscious reaction. I actually have to become conscious of this and slowly walk up the stairs now and "think happy thoughts" so I replace that negative feeling my body gets when I run up a flight of stairs. I also get this feeling when lying down at night. My heart pounds so heavily—that it in itself is frightening. It's almost as if my body is going into condition red, even in the absence of imminent danger.

One time while lying in bed next to my five-year-old, she coughed directly in my face, and my reaction even caught me off guard. I went from being relaxed to immediately angry and defensive and yelled at her. My wife saw what was happening and quickly took my daughter out of the room. I felt like I was being assaulted, and my body was getting ready for a fight. What followed was a feeling of anger, combativeness, and then sadness about everything. My heart began pounding, and I rocked myself to sleep. All this was triggered by a child's cough. As I mentioned before, sound is also a huge trigger for this reaction. Sometimes, I just feel like I need to fight something. I've considered buying a punching bag because I feel this primal need to fight.

This pent-up anger and aggression is making its way to my dreams at night. I feel like lately I am either screaming at someone or crying in my dreams. This often ends in my springing up in bed and shouting out loud. My dreams are often work based and involve me being on a call of some sort. More recently I had a dream someone was driving away from me while I was still in the window of their vehicle on a car stop. The car was literally dragging me and the operator did not care, as I am trying to grab at his neck. I jumped up in bed and yelled, "STOP THE [EXPLICIT] CAR!" I realized I did this immediately and tried to lie back down, but my wife had gotten scared and I felt her reach to check my pulse on my wrist.

Around this time, I wrote:

The most common feeling I have been getting lately is an overwhelming sadness that comes and goes, and I feel as though I need to cry for some reason but can't. I tend to have stretches of good days and bad days. The sadness is heavy and almost physical and more of an uncomfortable feeling than a thought. Sometimes fearful thoughts do still come in my mind as well, such as thoughts that I may die suddenly overnight and my wife will leave for work in the morning, leaving my children alone in the house with me dead in bed.

Sometimes, there were specific triggers that might bring on anxiety or a panic reaction.

One day, my mother-in-law, wife, kids, and I went to a farmer's fair. My daughter was riding the carnival rides when I noticed a young clean-shaven police officer who looked very fresh on the job and sharp. Looking at the detail officers, I tried to put myself back in the role for the moment and imagined myself in my cruiser going to a "hot call," lights and siren on, driving down the road. Suddenly, my heart begins to race and I start to feel panic and confusion, and I am hyperventilating. I am suddenly sweating, hot, and all the noises and lights around me—from the carnival rides clinking to the flashing gaudy lights and kids screaming—are magnified. The smell of overbuttered popcorn and grass from the field becomes pronounced and nauseating. I begin to feel sudden distrust and fear of everyone and smothered. What comes next is a sudden wave of sadness and then the realization that being a cop was over for me. Trying to hold back tears, I knew I needed to get out of there as fast as possible. I called my father-in-law to come and pick me up, leaving my wife, her mother, and the kids there.

As a police officer feeling suddenly weak and helpless, this is very difficult to swallow. The things that I have done, that you have read about, I don't think I could do those things anymore. I am not that person anymore. I feel weak, defeated, and I look back in sadness and wonder how this happened.

What happened to me?

* * * * *

I recently spoke with another officer, who had to retire from PTSD over two years ago. He had reached out to me by phone when he heard I was out of work from the same thing.

This officer was on patrol for a long time and was one of the most senior people there for time on the job. He was always quirky and jovial every morning at roll call, and though people found him a little strange in a Bill Nye, Mr. Roger's hybrid kind of way, he was genuinely a nice guy. He would always pick his area and assignments for the day, including that he was equipped with "a TASER weapon, smile, and banana." He was the last person I ever thought would become broken.

Since going through the same thing, I had wanted to reach out to him, as I knew he would understand what I was going through, but I didn't want to upset him or bother him.

When I spoke to him on the phone, I could tell he was still in a very vulnerable place as well. His PTSD had been very crippling. At times he felt "stupid," and he had difficulty performing even the simplest life tasks. He told me he felt as though the support from counseling was insufficient and that every therapist he spoke to only brought out more issues and made things worse. He ended up checking himself into in-patient rehab for several months among other first responders suffering from PTSD.

I would have to agree with him that talk therapy has also made me worse in some aspects, but then again, those buried issues that were dug up were bound to surface eventually. As we talked, we discovered similarities between our conditions, such as sensitivity to loud noise, moments of aggravation, and even the feeling that we've lost part of ourselves as the brave police officers we once were.

I don't know where he stands in his faith and beliefs, but I have told my own doctors and therapists that without mine, I would have been much worse.

> *O Lord, You brought my soul up from the grave;*
> *You have kept me alive, that I should not go down*
> *to the pit.*
> PSALM 30:3 NKJV

As I had mentioned earlier, I would be lying if I said my faith has not been tested during this process. I have, as I said before, questioned God more than ever. Is my search for salvation causing the enemy to attack me? I have experienced so much spiritual warfare during this time.

One morning after waking up, my mind began to wander in discomfort. I felt the very irking of lust accompanied by a sudden shake in faith, which both originated from my dreams.

I fear that just as God can enter our thoughts through our sleep, so can the enemy. I was careful not to entertain my thoughts too much and instead began to search for comfort in Scripture and by watching content from some of my favorite Christian leaders. After hearing the Word, I started reading where I had left off in the Gospels.

If you have read any of the Gospels, you know that several stories are repeated throughout with some new details in different accounts. Although I have seen the parable of the farmer spreading seeds before, today it had special meaning for me. Just like I had mentioned previously, the scripture of being corrupted and deceived by the serpent (2 Corinthians 11:3), this passage had again fit the perfect timing to my moment as if brought to me again on purpose. Read the words of Jesus in Luke 8:12–15:

> *"The seeds that feel on the footpath represent those who hear the message, only to have the devil come and take it away from their hearts and prevent them from believing and being saved. The seeds on the rocky soil represent those who hear the message and receive it with joy. But since they don't have deep roots, they believe for a while, then they fall away when they face temptation. The seeds that fall among the thorns represent those who hear the message, but all too quickly the message is crowded out by the cares and riches and pleasures of this life so they never grow into maturity. And the seed that fell on the good soil represent honest, good-hearted people who hear God's word, cling to it, and patiently produce a huge harvest."*

I find myself on occasion falling into the first two categories. What must I do to reach maturity? I want to be the seed that took root in fertile ground. I know this process is going to test me and I just have to continue pulling forward. I am not alone in this; many Christians struggle with the same, but we continue to be pulled back.

The same day, I was listening to a song by one of my favorite Christian rock bands, and one of the lyrics spoke to me about losing faith and God pulling you right back in again.

The next night, I have another dream.

A man driving a car gets in a serious car accident and is pulled out by a passerby. The passerby starts to go on that the man was saved only because of the grace and wonder of God. While the man is passionately talking about God, his eyes roll back in his head and he is in cardiac arrest on the ground and dies.

A few nights, later, I have another dream.

My wife and I are lying in bed, and there is this thing. I don't know what it is, but it is smaller than me, ugly, and I can't really describe it. It's not quite a monster, and it's not quite human. I can't really remember what it is, but it is irritating and annoying and it won't leave me alone. In fact, it keeps following me and it's now trying to get into bed with me. I am yelling at it to go away, but it won't and it continues to try to climb into bed with me and my wife. I'm getting so mad at this thing and repulsed by it. I threaten to call the police on it (ironic), but it won't go away. Finally, I take matters into my own hands, as it's persistently trying to climb onto bed and invade my space. The thing feels very evil all of a sudden; I grab the thing behind the neck in a choke hold and start squeezing to try to kill it. Suddenly, I feel an actual sharp pain in my side as if something very real is fighting me back, and I wake up.

Unfortunately, this was not the end to the dreams like these.

I woke up recently from my wife tapping me as I suddenly realized I was wrestling with my pillow, struggling to handcuff a combative suspect in my dreams. My psychiatrist eventually placed me on another medication, which was supposed to help with night terrors such as these, but more medication is just putting another bandage over the underlying issue.

I know that I am not alone in this struggle. I know that this all happened for a reason. I know that I am writing this book, which although may be terrible for the reader, is flowing from my mind. Scriptures I am coming across in my reads are just popping out, and they are applicable to what I am feeling and writing about.

In the current world we live in, evil is reigning supreme and only seems to be getting worse. What is up is now down and vice versa.

Those people belong to this world, so they speak from the world's viewpoint, and the world listens to them.

1 JOHN 4:5

We are even seeing some popular Christian leaders even walking away from their faith because it conflicts with the world we live in. These things both scare and concern me, but I have to remember that this was predicted and foretold by Jesus in Matthew 24: 9–10: "You will be hated all over the world because you are my followers. And many will turn away from me and betray and hate each other.".

How difficult will it be to raise my children in this world? They will be exposed to so much. We are no doubt experiencing the "birth pains" Jesus speaks of in Matthew 24 that depict his return is soon. As a police officer being among so much evil, I have always felt I was on the front lines of the end times. This, however, is not where I want to be and perhaps not where God wants me anymore either.

In the New King James Version of Matthew 24:12, Jesus says that there will be an increase in "lawlessness" in the last days, while other translations may use the word evil. This is a perfect example of why I think it's important to look at different translations of Scripture: Some are more applicable, and you may have noticed I use several different translations of Scripture throughout the book. In this particular instance, I prefer the NKJV because "lawlessness" illustrates what's happening to police officers around the country.

In the last few years, we have seen violent targeted attacks on police officers in which some were murdered. Currently at the time of writing this, police in New York City are being assaulted with garbage and buckets of water, yet the mayor does nothing. It has become acceptable to view us as the enemy. There are many narratives behind this mentality that portray police officers as murderers and thieves. While I have let you into our world and you have seen that as a Christian I don't always agree about the enforcement and fairness of certain laws and situations, without police there would be chaos. Being a police officer is difficult in today's world, and it has changed drastically since I got hired in 2007. I gradually saw things getting worse over time, and I pity the officers who are just getting hired and starting their career.

The last few years have proved especially difficult for police officers. The narrative of police as murders was abundant, and riots and protests have sprung up over the country from police-related shootings and tension-filled race relations. The media was pouring fuel over the flames and reporting things before most of the facts of the case were present, further dividing the line of trust. Officer-worn body cameras became both a blessing and curse and a public relations nightmare. Cops were targeted, killed, and assaulted for retaliation. We began to be painted as an enemy of the people. This was a strange time to go to work, but I did note an outpouring of support as a result of it as well.

Politics aside, no cop goes to work looking to shoot anyone. It's not worth being charged with murder or manslaughter and having to withstand all the agony, stress, and hardship that comes with a line-of-duty shooting. Officers are placed on leave, scrutinized by the public, media, and their own department as well, not to mention a jury of your "peers" (citizens who don't know anything about police work) in criminal and civil proceedings. This, if anything, deters officers so much from having to use lethal force that they may actually hesitate or be reluctant to pull the trigger when necessary.

There was a story in the last few years in which an officer failed to shoot an individual who was holding a large rock. The officer was eventually struck in the head by the suspect with the rock, and he died. His friends and family were outraged, as they felt everything going on in the media made him afraid to protect himself when he should have.

There is so much negative light on police nowadays that we have become the bad guys. The judicial system favors the real criminals, and the cops are the ones who end up standing trial. We are actually letting criminals off because of mistakes in police procedures. A murderer could walk free because an officer looked at a cell phone without a warrant. I am all for checks and balances and due process, but it has gotten out of control.

If we are truly getting closer to the second coming of Jesus, I don't want to be spending time as a seed on the wrong ground. I'd rather be close to my family, away from the widespread evil, instead of on the front lines of it.

I know faith is a battle, but I honestly feel those that never battle with it at all are not truly able to find closeness to God. Seeking out this closeness has come to show me that it requires seeking out and digging spiritually. It's OK to ask God those hard questions. I have done so recently, and in my quest for knowledge and understanding I've found some of the answers I've been searching for. At the same time, I have come to learn that we are also not meant to understand everything about God, nor are we capable of it.

CHAPTER 14

SALT IN THE WOUNDS: VICTIMIZING THE VICTIM, A BROKEN PROCESS

My speech and my preaching [were] in demonstration of the Spirit and of power: That your faith should not rest in the wisdom of men, but in the power of God.

1 Corinthians 2:5 KJV

When I attended the police academy, they had a special night where you invited your family to talk about the stressors of police work and life. This was a support night where several police officers, along with their family and spouses, sat on a panel. Then both the recruits and their family members were able to rotate through both groups separately and ask various questions about police life, police spouse and family life, and related stressors. They had a peer support specialist there to speak about PTSD and how being a police officer can change you and your family circle. The whole thing seemed rather promising and supportive at the time. The impression I got was that there was a system in place if police officers needed it for mental health reasons. Mind you, this was before active shooter incidents began increasing in frequency and way before the shooting at Sandy Hook Elementary on December 14, 2012.

Fast-forward twelve years, and police suicides are rampant across the country. There have been more police officer deaths by suicide at the time I am writing this in 2019 than that of any line-of-duty death this year. Why? Is it because we are just supposed to "suck it up"? No matter what we see repeatedly and get exposed to as cops, we are just supposed to let it build and build until we are both mentally and physically affected by it. But if a cop kills himself, then people want to ask questions. His peers will claim they never saw it coming.

There is too much silence on this issue; cops are ashamed and worried to come forward with their problems. It was the same reason I didn't talk to anyone initially when I started having problems looking at dead people: I feared it would cost me my job, or that I would be put on medication and labeled "crazy."

* * * * *

When I initially went out on work-related stress, none of my supervisors ever reached out to me to ask me if I was OK or to see how I was doing. I can tell you that I felt there was no support for me from my department. I only had one officer from the peer support reaching out to me, and I felt bad for him because he was becoming stressed out and overburdened by my issues. (Thank you by the way, if you are reading this.) I was talking only to the peer support team, and it appeared they were receiving much flack and being burdened by continuous questions from the administration.

"What's wrong with him?"

"How long is he going to be out?"

"We want details."

What they failed to understand was that I was entitled to privacy at that point.

At the very beginning I had one supervisor text me that I had not submitted any additional doctor's notes to him directly, and that I was not following chain of command because I had the peer support team submit the paperwork for me.

What they also failed to realize is that when you are suffering from PTSD, the last thing you need is any additional stress, and this is why the peer support officer was trying to assist. I was thinking, I should not have to be worrying about answering to this supervisor at this moment. Talk about making me feel more stressed out and worse. I want nothing to do with work because just the thought of work can trigger emotions.

The same supervisor also began giving me a little bit of hard time for not continuously submitting doctor's notes from appointment to appointment. They were treating my injury like a broken ankle, wanting the doctor to provide return-to-work dates and estimates. Mental illness clearly does not work that way, and they were adding additional stress on me when I was already in a very vulnerable state.

At the time, I very much believed that this was going to be declared an Injury on Duty, or IOD. I did not develop PTSD from anywhere else. Prior to being a police officer, I never had any mental health illness, and I, like every other officer, had to undergo substantial psychological testing and meet with a doctor as part of the hiring process to become a police officer.

Along with everything, I began to feel guilty and ashamed about what was going on. (I still feel this way—that nobody seems to understand what I'm going through.) I felt like I was being treated like a suspect of a crime. This manifested itself in my dreams.

One night, I had a dream that I drove into the back lot of

work, and because I was taking antidepressants, they arrested me for driving into work under the influence. In the dream, I was so upset and angry by the lack of support and the way they were treating me like a criminal, I started yelling, "YOU DID THIS TO ME!" as they dragged me away in handcuffs.

To make matters worse, the town human resources department starts sending me Family Medical Leave Act packets to fill out for "your own serious illness" in which they are requiring me to use my own personal sick and vacation time to get paid.

Filling out this paperwork is painful because it's like they are purposely denying my PTSD was caused by work, as if I just had an unrelated illness. I would meet with my clinician weekly, in addition to seeing my primary care doctor and the psychiatrist— all who diagnosed me with having severe PTSD due to my duties as a police officer—yet the town refused to accept any of this. I submitted multiple doctors' notes in support of all this; however, my personal time began to dwindle and I was ultimately forced to take an unpaid leave of absence. Now, on top of the symptoms of PTSD, not sleeping, the feeling of no support, I was going to worry about paying the bills. Does this all seem right to you?

I told my psychiatrist I never received any supportive texts or phone calls from anyone in the administration, and it deeply hurt me. I felt like I'd been dropped off of the face of the earth after twelve years of service, simply because I asked for help. Now that I am not longer "Officer Anthony" to them, I am a liability and an insurance claim that they will do everything in their power to not recognize. I feel abandoned and forgotten because I am broken, like everyone has turned against me. But I supposed that's how the enemy wanted me to feel.

* * * * *

*I am forgotten like a dead man, out of mind; I am like
a broken vessel. For I hear the slander of many; fear is
on every side; while they take counsel together against
me. ... But as for me, I trust in You, O LORD; I say,
"You are my God."*

PSALM 31:12-14 NKJV

They want to know why police suicide is so high. How do
you expect police officers to come forward if they are going to
be treated like this? Not only that, but every time I had to fill
out paperwork and jump through all kinds of hoops, they added
additional stress and worry about my future and my finances. *No
wonder I can't sleep at night! How am I supposed to heal from all this
if they keep adding additional stressors through the lack of support and
this treatment?*

My doctors told me they see this with all kinds of work
claims and that employers will do everything in their power to
deny them. I was sitting there in front of my psychiatrist literally
crying hysterically and angry at the same time about the way I was
being treated. My emotions and my "switch" in my brain are off
as it is, only being ever so slightly balanced by the high dose of
medication I am on. Why are they subjecting me to all this?

I recently found out they denied my claim without ever even
requesting my treatment records from my psychiatrist.

* * * * *

*Dear friends, don't be surprised by the fiery trials
you are going through, as if something strange were
happening to you. Instead, be very glad—for these
trials make you partners with Christ in his suffering,*

so that you will have the wonderful joy of seeing his glory when it is revealed to the world.
1 PETER 4:12-13

First Peter 4:12–13 is such an interesting scripture, and I discovered its importance only after reading about Jesus in the garden of Gethsemane before he was to be betrayed, captured, and crucified. This is a very touching moment; I needed to see Jesus' anguish and suffering at that moment.

Jesus was very aware of his fate from the beginning of his life, but it was not until this very moment in Matthew 26:38 where he tells his disciples, "My soul is deeply grieved, to the point of death" (NASB). The Bible says in Luke 22:42 that Jesus was so distressed that he fell to his face, praying, "Father, if you are willing, please take this cup of suffering away from me pass from me. Yet I want your will to be done, not mine." Verse 44 illustrates that Jesus was in such anguish that "his sweat was like drops of blood falling to the ground" (NIV).

When I first read this, I honestly began to cry myself—not for me but for Jesus. I honestly felt so moved and sad for him but also so grateful for what he had to endure for us.

This scripture also perfectly illustrates that Jesus knows suffering. He knows pain and grief. And more importantly, he knows about fear and death. Jesus was God, but he was also human, and he walked this earth, and with all his power he experienced human emotion. John 11:35 says that Jesus even wept when he heard the news of his friend Lazarus' death. Of course, he ended up raising Lazarus from the dead, but we see his human side illustrated in this moment as well.

I recommend anyone who is suffering from anxiety,

depression, or PTSD to read the moments leading to Jesus' death, and you will come away with a better understanding of why God the Father allowed him to suffer. Jesus suffered and endured pain not only for our sins, but I truly believe because of God's love for us, as faulted and broken as we are, and his desire to have the ultimate bond and relationship with us through his Son, Jesus.

I tell you this: I could not be sitting here typing about all this if it were not for the Lord. Only he has given me the strength to continue to wake up every day and push forward for myself and my family. As I write this, I am still so very uncertain about my future and my finances. I could sit here and think about that and literally drive myself crazy, but God protects me from that. I have been doing very well, not worrying about the future to the point where I can't function, and I take each day as it comes.

I have faith, and recently I had a feeling that the town was going to "concede." This was a very positive feeling, and it hit me while I was sitting in bed, going through one of my anxious moments. I know what the word concede means, but I felt like it popped into my mind when this positive feeling happened. So I looked up several definitions, and it generally means to give into something that was once denied. How perfect of a word to be given to me. So it is with hope and faith that I say the battle is already won. While we don't know the process or the timing, God wins in every scenario, even if the outcome is not the one we are expecting.

> "The Lord himself goes before you and will be with you; he will never leave you nor forsake you. Do not be afraid; do not be discouraged."
> DEUTERONOMY 31:8 NIV

Second Chronicles 20:15 tells us not to be afraid, "for the battle is not yours, but God's." I cannot try to fight this all on my own. I have to surrender to God and his will. I have to believe that what happens is what is right and best for me and his will. This can be a very hard thing to do, because you are putting all your trust in him. I ask you, though, what other choice is there? Sometimes, God has shown me I cannot do this alone. I have also learned through the course of all this that this process is making me a better person. These struggles may have caught me off guard initially and seemed confusing, but now I understand why I am going through it.

I believe by evidence of this very book that this process was meant to save me. While I am still struggling during this journey, I feel I am nevertheless still moving forward and making progress. I expect there will be setbacks, but as long as I kept the gear shifter in drive, I will continue forward.

CHAPTER 15

BATTLING AGAINST GOLIATH, FINDING FAVOR WITH GOD

For I have heard the slander of many, terror is on every side; while they took counsel together against me.
Psalm 31:13

As I write this in 2020, the New Year has begun, and I have been out of work for six months now. My matter has been set for arbitration (a trial basically) between the town and me to be heard in another six months from now. I had hoped that the union attorneys would try to settle the matter before this goes to arbitration. My faith is allegedly in the hands of a single person, an arbitrator, who is supposedly independent. I need to be strong in God and place my faith in him.

Lord, you are my lawyer! Plead my case!

"You have redeemed my life. You have seen the wrong they have done to me, Lord. Be my judge, and prove me right" (Lamentations 3:58–59).

I would resign from my job now and lose everything they owe me just to remove some of the burden, but I have to at least stick it out and see where it leaves me. I am then reminded to remember what Jesus went through in his final moments: "Think of all the hostility he endured from sinful people: then you won't become weary and give up" (Hebrews 12:3).

God willing, this matter will be miraculously resolved before I have to stand trial like a criminal and have the town's attorneys chastise me, making all kinds of claims against me. The Bible tells us in Luke 12:11–12 not to worry about how to defend ourselves because the Holy Spirit will guide us in that moment. In a way, I will be standing trial much like Jesus, Paul, and the apostles throughout the New Testament. Paul was continuously subjected to several trials throughout the book of Acts, and even he had to appeal to Caesar for his case to be heard in Rome. On the ship to Rome, Paul wrote in Acts 27:23–24, "Last night an angel of the God to whom I belong and whom I serve stood beside me, and he said, 'Don't be afraid, Paul, for you must surely stand trial before Caesar! What's more, God in his goodness has granted safety to everyone sailing with you."

Even if everyone else is a liar, God is true. As the Scriptures say about him, "you will be proved right in what you say, and you will win your case in court" (Romans 3:4).

Standing trial is part of being a Christian. My persecution is designed to make me stronger. I said to myself while lying in bed last night that if this suffering is designed to increase my faith and relationship with God, then so be it. I am meant to be a messenger for PTSD and God. And this book is meant to be a light for others.

"In the same way, let your light shine before others, so that they may see your good works and give glory to your Father who is in heaven" (Matthew 5:16 ESV).

It is easy to be worried; we still have bills to pay, a mortgage, car payments, and two small girls to feed. We had to start rearranging our lives. We sold our house and moved down south to be closer to family. We have made some major life changes, but we still have a lot to worry about, and a lot to figure out about our future. Much is at stake: how long my case will go, finding new jobs, and of course surviving financially. I wonder what jobs there will be for a medically retired police officer, and whether prospective employers will label me as "unhireable" due to my mental health diagnosis.

I have to try to take each day, each moment as it comes, for God says in Psalm 32:8, "I will guide you along the best pathway for your life. I will advise you and watch over you." As extremely difficult as this is, going forward I have to remind myself daily to not worry about the future. And let me tell you, uncertainty is extremely difficult to bear, and there are days where I just feel completely overwhelmed with worry and panic, and the enemy capitalizes on it.

I am also very angry with the town for what they are putting me through, but I cannot dwell on anger either, for the Bible says in James 1:20, "Human anger does not produce the righteousness God desires." Being angry about my situation is not going to change anything; it only causes me additional grief and adds to my burdens. I am not preaching to you, reader. Trust me, I am greatly struggling with worry about my future. My reading Scripture and typing this is to reaffirm what God promises, if I keep my eyes on him. Faith is a struggle, and I yearn for the place in my life to be stronger in it.

"So do not worry about these things, saying 'What will we eat? What will we drink? What will we wear?' ... Your heavenly Father already knows all your needs. Seek the kingdom of God above all else, and live righteously, and he will give you everything you need. So don't worry about tomorrow, for tomorrow will bring its own worries. Today's trouble is enough for today" (Matthew 6:32).

Regardless of the outcome, I have to believe that what has happened to me was all meant for my good. There has been some good that has come out of it already. I have more time with my children. Working in law enforcement has often meant being away and working on birthdays and holidays, and I have had the joy to experience both this year with the kids while they are still small. Childcare has also not been an issue anymore, and my oldest daughter is able to attend preschool five days a week without us having to worry about finding childcare and different conflicting schedules. My being home has added balance and consistency to the children's lives and our home. Above all, I have come so much closer to finding understanding in God, to which this book is a testament.

Trust me, at times looking back at this book, doing some editing, it's like reading someone else's work. And I have come to realize that I did not write this book myself—it was guided by the Holy Spirit. I am not a Bible scholar, but Scripture has jumped out at me, and I was able to apply it when needed in the text and organize it in a way that makes sense and can be understood (at least I think I did). Again, while this is meant to teach and help me, I believe it is also meant to deliver the message to you, the reader. Not everyone will pick up a Bible and casually read through it. For most people, Scripture is only heard if one attends church, and I find delivery of it sometimes can be inconsistent or not put in a way that is applicable to real life. Scripture is best understood in one's personal study of the Bible or in the context of a story.

* * * * *

While sitting in the waiting room before a visit with my psychiatrist in spring 2020, I received an email from the union. One of our officers, a nice guy, decided he was going to leave early and start at another department somewhere else. This officer was still on the books with our department until the end of the month. I learned in the email that he decided to donate his remaining sick time to me, almost six months' worth of time to me, which would at least take me to June. I was so happy, I texted my mother and my wife, and both of their responses were, "WHAT!?" I praised God, as did my mother and wife. The week before I had just increased my tithes, and as a thank-you and a leap of faith, I decided to up my monthly tithe even more.

A week later, I was still not getting paid, and I received a call from a union representative at work, who told me that the town manager was trying to deny the sick time that was donated to me. People had donated sick time to other officers in the past, without any problems, but never this large of an amount. The union rep advised that after he went to the town administration office, he got the impression the town administration was toying with me.

The town administration was trying to argue that since the first of the year, I had accrued more vacation time than I could use; however, the union did not believe I had accrued time while on unpaid leave. He then stated that I would have to expend those vacation days first, then he said it would be too late for me to use the donated sick time because the detective would officially be off the town books and payroll. I can guarantee this: Had I not had this sick time donated, and I tried to use the "newly accrued" vacation time for pay, the town would have denied that as well, saying that we don't accrue time on unpaid leave.

I know this was the work of the devil trying to upset me, entering the mind of the town officials, who were purposely trying to block me from getting the sick time donated.

* * * * *

Three weeks then went by since the union spoke to the administration. I had asked the union what was going on with the situation. The union rep contacted me back and said the town administration would give him an answer the following Tuesday.

Well, that Tuesday came and went with no answer. The next day I inquired about the situation again, and the union rep told me he called the town manager three times and was not calling him back. I can't but help but get the impression this was a stall tactic. The town may be much greater than me; they may win some battles. But they will not win the war.

> *David replied to the Philistine [Goliath], "You come against me with sword, spear, and javelin, but I come against you in the name of the LORD of Heaven's Armies. ... This is the LORD's battle, and he will give you to us!"*
> 1 SAMUEL 17:45, 47

The following day I received a call from the union rep. He stated that the town administration said that they were going to deny the sick time donation and they do not believe I accrued vacation time either, but they may allow me to have accrued twenty or so days of vacation, which will only last me a month.

I was confused; it didn't make sense. I said, "Wait a minute, their argument is that I accrued vacation and I have to use that first, so I can't use the sick time donation. Now they are saying they might allow me to use vacation. It's either one or the other. If I did not accrue vacation the first of the year being on unpaid leave, then I qualify for the sick time donation, which it says in our collective bargaining agreement can be used if you have no more paid time."

The town, in my opinion, was clearly manipulating things

and making them up as they saw fit. The union indicated that the town "did not want to go to another arbitration over this," as it would cost them a large sum of money.

When I got off the phone, I was so upset, but not at God—I still trust him in what is going on. I was just getting so frustrated over the unnecessary torment. Both the union and the attorneys commented they did not understand why the town was being so incredibly difficult.

> *Pharaoh's heart, however, remained hard. He still refused to listen, just as the LORD had predicted.*
> EXODUS 7:13

After being denied the use of the donated sick time, I was "allowed" to use the vacation time I had accrued from the first of the year, which lasted me a few weeks. My temporary disability also ran out, and in spring 2020 we began relying on my wife's salary and our savings.

After a month or so had gone by, I went to go see my psychiatrist, who finished compiling her completed medical evaluation. What she had presented to the town was nothing short of an extremely well-detailed report that linked several episodes of trauma, many of which you have read about in this book, and tied them to all the symptoms I had been experiencing. She also stated that she did not recommend I return to work as a law enforcement officer.

After the union attorneys reviewed the medical report, they suggested I file for a service-connected disability with the town and had me draft up a letter of application. Writing this letter for me was a very emotional experience, as the reality sunk in that I was no longer going to be a cop anymore. I was, in essence, retiring. I ended the letter to the town manager by stating that I was proud to have served as a police officer for twelve years, and I believed I served the public with empathy, honesty, and integrity and thanked him for the opportunity to serve.

Another month passed after I filed my letter, and there was no communication from any of the department command staff, my attorneys, or the town. My attorney initially said, after reading the doctor's medical report, that it would be "completely ridiculous" for the town to still want to pursue the matter. Unfortunately, after inquiring about the status of my letter, I was told by the union that the town was planning to deny the retirement.

The good news is, my doctor's report is very solid. The attorney said to me in all of his thirty years fighting work-related injury cases, he has never seen a doctor's report as detailed and well written as mine. The attorney flat-out stated it was "the most well-written medical report" he has ever seen.

* * * * *

Praise Jesus, and thank you for your favor, "for you bless the righteous, O Lord; you cover [them] with your favor as with a shield" (Psalm 5:12 ESV).

As righteous people, God will grant us favor in many things in life. Favor among our peers, favor among our employers, and even favor with doctors and medical staff if needed. Even people who are not believers will be able to see the light of God inside of you. They may not know why they are so eager to help and support you, but nevertheless they will be your advocates. We will also have people and forces that will come against us, but God has placed others in our path to favor us.

During this process of working with my doctors and different people, I have seen God's favor come through. Throughout the lengthy and irritating process of filing for temporary disability from the state, people often complain about the red tape and attitudes they encounter in what is already a difficult and stressful time in their life. Upon calling the disability hotline, however, I encountered a lovely woman on the other end who went out of her way to help me, even saying, "We are going to take care of it, honey," and she gave me her own personal extension in case I had any problems.

God touches people unbeknownst to them to place them on your team and give you favor. I must say both of my doctors and my clinician have treated me with what I feel was an "above and beyond" level of care and were truly looking out for my best interests and not treating me like just another patient. God made this clear in the doctor's final medical report.

I am realizing now more than ever that our actions and lives are to be aligned with God's before this favor can be displayed. If you notice Psalm 5:12, it says God blesses the "righteous" (or the "godly" according to other translations). In other words, we have to live according to God's will for us to receive favor and blessing. People sometimes think that because Jesus died on the cross, all our sins—past and present—are forgiven. While it is true that Jesus was the final blood sacrifice for our human sin, this is not an excuse to continue to commit sin, thinking there are no consequences.

I like to use the example of my five-year-old daughter. When she does something wrong, she always cries, "Forgive me!" While I will always forgive just as Jesus will always forgive us, she seems to be under the impression that she could repeat the behavior next time and just ask for forgiveness again. While this may be comical coming from a rather intelligent five-year-old trying to manipulate her parents, it parallels our life on earth as sinners. I, too, can be guilty of the same actions: in the past I would repeat the same sin, feel guilty about it, then ask for forgiveness.

It is not enough to simply say, "Lord, forgive me," then continued to repeat the same sin. You have to at least try to change directions. If you stumble and fall, try and try again until you master the sin. If you liken it to someone with an addiction, at some point, hopefully, that person will say "enough is enough" and change directions. It's possible they may relapse. God willing, they won't, but if they do, they must continue on the path until they overcome their addiction. I really do believe God recognizes the attempt, just like he recognizes faith.

God doesn't expect us to be completely sin-free; we are of the flesh, and our flesh is of "original sin." God's original design for man was sinless, but in his love for us, he gave us free will, and man chose sin, forever clothing us in sinful flesh. Of course, through Jesus' sacrifice, we are free from the original sin, but our personal sins still affect us. I believe sin not only affects our minds but also our physical health and our relationships with others. Being righteous is our attempt to mirror God and live by his law.

"Imitate God, therefore, in everything you do, because you are his dear children. Live a life filled with love, following the example of Christ. ... So be careful how you live. Don't live like fools, but like those who are wise. Make the most of every opportunity in these evil days" (Ephesians 5:1–2, 15–16).

Notice the wording in the first verse of Ephesians 5: We are to "imitate" God. The book of Ephesians—as well as the other letters in the New Testament—serves as a good starting point for anyone new to the Bible. I call these books combined "the instruction manual" because they give such detailed instructions on how to live righteously—everything from sexual immorality no-no's to rules within a marriage. After reading these books, it perplexes me how modern-day people, especially some Christians (and churches!), make excuses or justify certain social norms that are written about in the Bible.

After my journey with PTSD, I have especially come to realize that a lot of Christians, regardless of denomination, do not actually read the Bible, as if it were outdated or removed from norm. I was amazed at how much actual content is in there and how applicable it is to everyday and current times. If you want to undertake the issue of reading the Bible, get yourself an easy-to-read translation, such as the New Living Translation, which is not written in Old English and is easier to digest for the average person.

I would personally say, save the Old Testament for after you have read and understood the New Testament. The Old Testament can be very intimidating and is filled with laws that fall under the old covenant with God's people that were later fulfilled differently with Jesus' birth, death, and resurrection. You also have to take into context the mentality and type of people who lived rather simply and savagely back then to understand why God worked the way he did with them. I admit that I myself had a lot of questions after I began to look at Old Testament stories. The Old Testament, however, does reveal certain prophecies about the future, and it is really cool to see predictions from prophets like David, Isiah, and Daniel later fulfilled in the New Testament.

Do yourself a favor: Pick up a Bible and actually read it, and I promise you will find what you are looking for.

CHAPTER 16

A PLAGUE, A PASSOVER, AND AN AWAKENING

"If my people, who are called by my name, will humble themselves and pray and seek my face and turn from their wicked ways, then I will hear from heaven, and I will forgive their sin and will heal their land."

2 CHRONICLES 7:14

As I am writing this in March 2020, we are going through a critical time in our history. A true Passover has taken place over the world in the form of "coronavirus." This pandemic we are currently in by no coincidence coincided with Lent, Passover, and Jesus' death and resurrection. As we wait in darkness of this potentially deadly disease, I am reminded of the darkness I have experienced over the past year. People everywhere are in great fear and experiencing severe anxiety, as we are quarantined in our houses.

Considering my fear of death, which I have struggled with in the past, you would think I would be terrified as well. I would like to report, however, I am at great peace—now more than ever, in fact. Yes, I have no income from work; and at the time of this writing, we were in the process of selling our home and moving to Florida. Our house was on the market one day, and we had a buyer with a good offer, but they backed out weeks later. There are currently travel restrictions, the real estate market has completely frozen, and my wife and I are seeking jobs in a rapidly declining, halted economy. Am I worried?

No.

I was talking to God about this book and everything currently going on, wondering when everything would come to pass with my retirement and our future, and he said to me, I know the timing.

* * * * *

I set up a Facebook account during my college years, but I never used it. That is, until this Lenten season, when I felt a call to take to Facebook and use it as a tool to preach the word. I felt God was telling me, *You will go forth and preach the word and gather my children.* I also felt a promise in my heart that God would "deliver" us to a better life and that he had a "hand-made job" for me. Since Lent has started, every day God has been leading me to messages in the Word, and I have posting them to my Facebook story.

During my trips to the grocery, I encountered many people walking around with such a sense of impending doom. An elderly woman wiping down her cart looked at me and said, "They say for people my age, this is the angel of death." As someone who is overcoming fear—you have read about the devil's attacks in this area throughout Invisible Wounds—I know the fear these people are facing. I can't help but feel now is the time more than ever to bring people to God. Jesus said, in regards to the end of times:

- "But this will be your opportunity to tell them about me" (Luke 21:13).
- "I say, wake up and look around. The fields are already ripe for harvest" (John 4:35).

During this pandemic, I feel God has been using me and other Christians to reach out to the rest of our family and friends. I am not someone who is big into posting other people's Bible memes. I like to be led by the Word and make my own depending on the day, almost like a daily devotional.

I am so amazed and overjoyed that I am not experiencing the fear which has overcome the world right now. I am also very glad that as a police officer I am not exposed more than I need to be to both the virus and to death, because God removed me from there before all this.

* * * * *

I said before that I believed God was protecting me from something. One of my biggest fears was seeing a deceased child while on duty as a police officer.

Recently while visiting my psychiatrist, I told her of a dream I had. In the dream I responded to a call for a missing toddler. In the dream, it was pouring rain, and after I searched the area, I located the child, who was facing down in water, deceased. In the dream, I experienced such real anguish and was crying hysterically, saying, "I can't do this anymore!" I told the doctor I never went on a call like this, and was I wondering why I was having dreams about things that never happened at work versus things that did. My doctor said, "Sometimes we dream about our deepest fears," and left it like that.

Two days ago, as of wiring this, I learned that officers on my shift responded to a call for a missing toddler in what would have been my usual assigned area. While on scene, the officers located the child, facedown in a pool, deceased. I cried when I found this out. I could not believe it; my dream had come true, yet God saved me from that experience. I don't believe that I can predict the future in my dreams, but I am convinced God was showing me something. I knew that as a father of two small children, going on a call like that would have broken me.

We don't understand why God works the way he does or even why this child was allowed to die. I am not even sure why God was allowing me to see it in that dream (maybe as confirmation that he was saving me from that). This also begs the question, Why spare me from that, Lord, and not others? Why did you choose to remove me from policing? What is my intended purpose going forward that I was worth sparing? I can only imagine at this point, but I truly believe he has something good and exciting planned for me, and my purpose will always involve serving him as well.

That morning after reading the press release emails from work, I texted my clinician, who said she was actually on the way to the department to counsel the officers involved. I am glad to see that after my leave from work due to PTSD, the department is finally taking proactive steps. I don't know what they will do for the officers, but whether or not the officers want help, the department should give them paid time off to process the incident. I pray for them, and I pray for all police, EMS, nurses, doctors, and firefighters around the world that are exposed to so much trauma and death.

Even now, those like my wife, a registered nurse, is working among coronavirus patients. She is walking and breathing among them and coming home at night to our house. Am I afraid?

No, I am not.

I have plead the blood of our Savior, Jesus, over our house and anointed our door with oil. The plague is passing over, but "no evil will conquer you: no plague will come near your home" (Psalm 91:10).

* * * * *

Sadly, my time in law enforcement has come to an end. I do believe that when God closes one door, another one opens, and everything happens for a divine reason. I do hope, though, that I will have the opportunity to keep working in law enforcement in some capacity. My passion is teaching tactics and firearms, and I truly believe God has gifted me with public speaking. I am excited to see what he has in store for me. I don't know what my future holds, but I know it will be bright.

I pray that God continues to strengthen me in the path toward righteousness. I pray that the world wakes up and recognizes the evil around us. And I pray for those held captive to have freedom from fear and the grip of the enemy, in Jesus' name, Amen.

AFTERWORD

We were crushed and overwhelmed beyond our ability to endure, and we thought we would never live through it. In fact, we expected to die. But as a result, we stopped relying on ourselves and learned to rely only on God, who raises the dead.

2 CORINTHIANS 1:8-9

I had been dreading the trial for months. But like all things, it came and passed. The trial lasted a total of three long days, each separated by a month or so in between. The first day, both my attorney for the police union and the town's attorney presented their opening statements. Of course, this very book you are reading was not out yet, and because of my social media activity, the town was very aware I was writing it. Through my online presence, I became very vocal about my dealings and struggles with PTSD at the time, as meeting others in the same situation brought healing and a voice for me. I also did not want to feel ashamed about what I was going through, and talking about my experience was the only way to draw attention to the larger problem in law enforcement.

To set things up for you, imagine a room in which the arbitrator was seated in the middle, and to the left was the police union representative and my union attorney, while to the right was the town manager, the town's attorney, and the chief of police. Right there I felt as if the statement was being made right off the bat, whether by default or not, that the chief of police was on the town's side—not mine. Then there was me, the subject of this whole proceeding, the one like a criminal on trial. Due to the

COVID-19 pandemic, I was unable to travel to the location of the hearing, so I was brought in by online video conference. I thank the Lord for this, because I did not want to have to travel and endure all this alone.

Upon hearing the town's opening statement, I felt as their attorney's mission was clear. His goal was to paint me as a money hungry liar who was looking for an early retirement and was out to land a book deal. The town's attorney mentioned that during the trial they would see that I didn't meet "the high standard" of the law and that they would be providing an "expert witness" who would testify I did not meet the diagnostic criteria for PTSD. He then spoke about how he would be playing a podcast that I was featured on about my upcoming book in which I spoke in a "rather bragatory manner" about my accomplishments as a police officer. I'm pretty sure bragetory is not an actual word, but those are his words, not mine. Now, while writing this, I have to remind myself not to speak evil from my tongue, but I am also going to tell you some of the things that were said in this trial to illustrate, from my point of view, the flawed logic surrounding PTSD and how municipalities will stop at nothing to deny you benefits.

The first day began with my psychiatrist (I refer to her as "my doctor") being called to testify, also by teleconference. She is a well-established psychiatrist who attended medical school and began her career both abroad and then later here in America. My doctor has treated several first responders for PTSD from agencies for well over a decade. During her testimony, the town's attorney went over her professional history and tried to point out that she had not done any recent research or been published in the field of PTSD treatment. To this, my doctor responded that her ongoing clinical experience and current active role in the field had prevented her from doing any recent academic work. She also stated her experience made it unnecessary. I thought she handled herself well overall, but you could see she was not used to testifying. The town's attorney then pulled some rather dirty tricks and asked my doctor if she was "aware" that I had "lied" to her and whether that would change her opinion or diagnosis of me.

As I was sitting there both angry and shocked, I could not even fathom how he was going to say that I had lied to her. The attorney then stated that in one of my reports to my doctor I had stated that I lost a significant amount of weight, but records from recent visits to my primary care physician showed that I had gained weight each appointment in the last year.

Now let me be clear here: I knew that the town's attorney was manipulating the timeline of my weight loss and gain in order to confuse my doctor. A few years prior to me leaving work on leave from the PTSD, I had lost a significant amount of weight (over sixty pounds). I mentioned earlier in the book that at the time, I had also been suffering from severe acid reflux, which contributed to the weight loss, and in retrospect I suspect the acid reflux was due to the PTSD. Of course, before even all that happened, I had begun losing weight by changing my diet and working out in general, but it wasn't until the reflux that it became unhealthy.

The year that I was out of work, the pandemic was going on, and I was feeling down on myself, so yes, I did gain weight from a lot of emotional eating, thus my weight gain. What upset me, though, was the deceptive attempt to twist doctor's records. Thankfully my attorney was able to set the record straight.

The town's attorney continued to selectively pick things out of all of the different doctor's reports and intentionally leave out important information. He had commented that the day I had gone into the emergency room the day after I left work sick, the ER report read something to the wording of "patient is a "33 year old male, appears to be healthy." He then used this as basically the doctor's conclusion and findings. My attorney then read what was left out of the report of the symptoms I was suffering, my mention to the ER doctor of being a police officer, and my fear, as well as her subsequent prescribing of lorazepam.

I honestly could not believe what was going on, and it was extremely frustrating sitting there in silence, praying against all the lies and deception under my breath. At one point, he even accused my doctor of practicing unethically because she had concluded my PTSD was worked related. This statement made both my attorney and the arbitrator very uncomfortable, as my attorney objected to that statement, which was sustained.

Later in her testimony, the town's attorney asked, "Doctor, were you aware that Officer Anthony relocated and drove to Florida?" To my surprise he started a line of questioning that insinuated that if I had PTSD, I would not be able to drive a car or be able to do anything like write a book, as apparently I was supposed to just curl up in a ball in the corner.

Thankfully, my doctor responded, "That's not how PTSD works."

In another argument, he mentioned that I was an avid "firearms enthusiast" and questioned how I could look at guns if I had PTSD.

If you remember, earlier in the book I talked about how a certain brand of undershirts gave my anxiety when I would see them. While I did eventually throw them out, there were times I avoided anything to do with policing, but I realized I had to come out of that and face these things.

My doctor then testified that not everyone is triggered by the same things, advising that she has one responder whose anxiety is triggered by his boots.

"His boots?" the town's attorney mocked with skepticism.

On a quick side note, a friend once explained to me why things like undershirts and boots tend to be triggers. This is because these are usually the first articles of clothing you put on when dressing to start you day and shift at work. Makes sense, doesn't it?

When the next court date came, I had my chance to testify. I was extremely nervous, but the Lord gave me unbelievable strength and wisdom. I felt like for the most part, I was talking circles around the town's attorney, and he had zero argument to what I had to say, that is because no one knows better than me what I went through and I have and always been telling the truth. I don't think I have ever been so quick on my feet with answers and able to trap someone in deceit as I was that day. Thanks to the Lord, my brain was firing on all cylinders and that day was a tremendous victory for me both spiritually and for my recovery.

The funny part was prior to being cross examined the town's attorney says to me, "Before we begin, you understand I have a certain role to play in this, right?" I was not sure if he was just trying to save face with the arbitrator, God, or me, but he made sure to say that before he began.

Toward the end of my cross-examination, he says to me, "You said in the podcast, you were tired of fighting. Are you tired, Nick?"

At this point, I was very much on fire like I had just taken him down and was holding him by the sword. I responded, "You know, I was, but I just discovered a newfound strength." I ended by saying, this was not just about money or me, and that I would keep fighting for this cause regardless of the outcome.

To my surprise, at the end of my cross examination, he says to me something in the manner of, "I applaud you for your newfound faith and for fighting for your cause."

My thought was, *Whatever helps you sleep at night.*

The last day of trial, they brought forward their "expert witness," a doctor who does not actually treat patients but reviews medical claims and cases for a government agency. I did some research on this guy, and a quick online search shows he was no stranger to controversy, as allegedly he was suspected of some shady business, and both his home and office were raided in 2018 by the FBI. Of course, while they were quick to bring up that my clinician had a violation in her licenses, which accidently lapsed seven years ago, this, however, was not brought up in trial. I am told that in between break my attorney approached the town's attorney about this, and his response was, "Yeah, but he was never charged with anything."

Much to no surprise, he has never treated any first responders for PTSD, but cited that he once had a coast guard pilot that he saw. Let's not forget, he has also never seen or spoken a word to me as well, so his opinion should realistically hold no weight. He also said I did not meet any of the criteria outlined in the DSM (*Diagnostic and Statistical Manual of Mental Disorders*) one of which very clearly mentions things like being in danger and "first responders handlings remains" as just examples but they are not limited to this.

However, this "expert" (who by the looks of him never did anything physical or dangerous in his life) had the nerve to say that I, a veteran cop of twelve years, "have never been in danger." Now you have read the book, you be the judge of that one. He also stated that despite the over 30 incidents of me dealing with human remains, which included suicides, some of which you have read, where "not what the manual was referring to" saying that what it really was referring to was "incidents like September 11th," even though it does not say that. He also testified that I showed no signs of PTSD, such as nightmares, attention problems, and/or angry outbursts. I'll let you be the judge of that one as well. Lastly, despite me never having any history of mental health, he concluded that my doctor misdiagnosed me and that I must have been suffering from another issue or past trauma.

During his testimony, I wanted to scream, I was so annoyed, so angry as this paid actor, who sat there and got paid no doubt very well to essentially lie. I even caught him in a lie as he began to testify about my "facial expressions" that I made while I was being interviewed on the podcast I was featured on. The funny part was, it was an audio podcast only. When he said this, I lost it and was shaking my head and jumping in my seat. This got the town's attorney's attention, and he said, rather irked, "What's he shaking his head about? I want to know what he is saying over there."

I exploded. "HE'S LYING! WHAT FACIAL EXPRESSIONS? IT WAS AN AUDIO PODCAST!" I then added, "I'M SORRY, BUT THIS IS RIDICULOUS. YOU WANT TO SEE AN ANGRY OUTBURST? WELL, HERE IT IS."

Suddenly everyone in the room was quiet and looking at me. The town attorney then clarified that it was indeed an audio podcast.

And they moved on from it, as if nothing had happened.

"Whoever speaks the truth gives honest evidence, but a false witness utters deceit.

PROVERBS 12:17 ESV

To end the day, the town brought up three more witnesses to testify against me: my three supervisors. I don't know if this was an effort to pit them against me, but I don't blame the supervisors, they just answered questions and at the end of testimony had nice things to say about me as a person and a worker. To sum up the entire argument of the attorney, his claim was that I never displayed signs of issues to my supervisors and that nothing that I experienced was beyond the scope or job description and duties of a police officer. This last statement I even agreed with during my own testimony. The thing with PTSD however is not to judge the severity of someone's perceived trauma but instead look at how it affected them. Who are you to tell me what I saw was not severe enough? The idea that one's trauma is more significant than another's is so flawed and wrong. The other idea that exposure to danger and trauma is an inherent part of a police officer's job doesn't mitigate or deflect from the town's responsibility to take care of you when injured mentally or physically in the line of duty. That mentality is the like saying, "If an officer is shot in the line of duty, the town has no obligation because, well, it was part of your job description and you knew the inherent danger." Do you see the flawed argument here? PTSD is an injury and it should be treated as such, that's why more and more it is being referred to as PTSI, with the "I" meaning injury rather than disorder.

* * * * *

Here we are now, the beginning of 2021 as I write this. The other day, I had gotten the call regarding the outcome and destiny of this trial. I will say that I was caught off guard from this call, because the arbitrator's decision was not due to later in the month. The decision was in favor of the town, I lost the case, or should I say, we lost the case, because this is going to affect more people than just me.

To make matters even worse, the enemy wanted to further torment me as I was told the town administrator said that he was going to order me back to work or I would be fired. I laughed immediately when I heard this. The enemy will not win, my intention was to now retire under normal circumstances and at this point, the town stills owes me for the years of service I have put in. Neither the town administrator nor the enemy behind him will rob me of my past, my service, or God's glory.

I thought this would just be an administrative process to resign, but the enemy attacked again. After I requested to resign normally, months began to pass by. I would email, call, and request a status, but failed to get a response. Suddenly one day, I was notified that an hour or so of my video arbitration hearing—including my Doctor's testimony—appeared on the town's official social media page. The police union acted quickly and approached the town to have it taken down, but it was very suspicious. The town officials said they did not know how it got uploaded, but the more important question was: why was it recorded and saved in the first place? In this particular case, a stenographer was present for the official record; therefore nothing should have been recorded.

After not receiving an answer from my last status inquiry, the Police union drafted a letter to the town requesting an answer. They eventually responded with a pension board meeting (even though, to my understanding, this has never been the case before). Then, during the meeting via video conference, the town administrators attempted to say that I would not get the normal vested percentage of my base salary because I did not work my last year since I was out on unpaid leave. They claimed I was only entitled to a vested percentage of what I made the year I was out without pay, which was peanuts.

Of course, at this point in my spiritual journey, I am no longer the naïve sheep I once was and I knew that this was the enemy attacking. I knew the town administrators were merely a tool and they—as Jesus put it— "know not what they do." Even these ones in particular probably did, but the enemy can also blind and harden hearts. Either way, I have come to a great peace about things like this, as like everything else, I can give them to God to work out exactly how they are supposed to.

I had been praying for God's outcome rather than what I had wanted or thought I had wanted. I am disappointed more that justice and truth did not win in this case, but God cares more about me and my future than the outcome of a trial for financial benefits. I am not mad at God and believe that it is possible that winning the case would have forever tied me to a disability pension always looming over me and could have closed doors on any future opportunities for me based on my skillset. I have to trust God that he already knows what is best for me and this wasn't it. Know this though, I am not done on my journey for fighting this cause, and no court determines or rules on what I have struggled, my faith, or my future.

I believe I am at a better place spiritually now than when I started this book. I personally feel that I have made a lot of progress—mentally, physically and spiritually. I can look back now and feel like I accomplished a lot that I should be proud of in the twelve years I served. I know I made a difference in the lives of some citizens as well as officers.

During my time at the department, my passion was always training and the tactical evolution of my police department. I felt there was a gap in training from the military to the police world, and police were not always on the same level of preparedness as we all should be. I made it a mission of mine to better myself through training in tactical emergency medicine and considered myself solely responsible for making advanced tactical trauma care training available to every officer. I went from being told, "We don't need that training" to eventually almost every officer carrying a tourniquet on his or her belt. I was able to get us trauma kits for all the frontline cars, and I know that I also inspired other officers to be better prepared. I was eventually able to bring this training even to the civilian world and have personally trained well over a hundred civilian employees, including school teachers, in emergency trauma care.

What I consider to be one of my best achievements was getting selected to be a firearms instructor for the department. I expressed interest in this when I first got on the job, but was told by some that it would never happen. I took my position as firearms instructor seriously and always made sure to stay active and up to date. Each year I personally attended several training courses paid for with my own money, because the department never wanted to spend any money on continuing education. After every training I attended, I always made sure to bring that knowledge back to the officers of the department. I knew many did not have the same level of training that I did and that they weren't going to go seek it out on their own. I was also a firm believer that officers need to trust the skill of the other officers next to them, and sometimes that just wasn't the case when it came to shooting and tactics. But truth be told, it was not their fault—no one ever taught them.

When I became an active shooter instructor, I exhausted myself planning and setting up what I believed to be the best active shooter training the department had ever seen. I searched for training sites, planned extensively, and coordinated with the local fire department and volunteers to create one of the most intense and realistic experiences for the officers, short of the real thing. I may have not been the best street cop, but I can look back and know that the training I provided for the other officers was my legacy.

As I work my way through this new life outside of policing, I have found a sense of purpose and a form of therapy by going public with my story. First, I have met several people through the internet and have spoken with other officers and first responders throughout North America who also suffer from PTSD. This has shown me I am not alone. The Lord has led me to meet some people who have already had a positive impact on my life. Second, through some of these connections, I received training in Critical Incident Stress Debriefing, a method to help people work through initial trauma, and got certified as a law enforcement chaplain. Third, I have also been asked to volunteer in a peer support role for an organization that helps first responders with PTSD. Overall, I have made it a mission of mine to draw awareness to this issue and help other responders recognize and battle PTSD.

When this book gets published, I hope it serves a beacon of light against fear and depression for responders who have PTSD. You see, PTSD is weird: One minute you can be fine and the next minute curled up in a ball, rocking. At times, I could think about work without a problem, and at other times, strangely enough I could look at a police officer passing by or see an article of clothing from work and start having a panic attack or oppressive feelings. For some reason, writing about work felt very cathartic but afterward could bring up feelings later in the day that were not always good.

The good news is that God is a healer; He can mend any wound. I am happy to say I no longer suffer from the majority of these issues and I ONLY have God to thank. God is almighty and full of glory. He carried me through to a new chapter for a new purpose. He is your advocate, your doctor and most of all, your father; he loves you. If you give your life to him, as I did, then things will begin to turn in your favor and work out for your good. God loves every one of us and sometimes we need to be shaken to be awakened.

The enemy will tell you lies, but God always tells you the truth. Sadly, Police and responder suicides are an issue in this nation. I never want to judge anyone in that mindset or that position, but if you are seeking God and aligning yourself with him, then evil thoughts of harm should never be allowed to take root and grow. 2 Corinthians 10:5 NIV says that we must "take captive every thought to make it obedient to Christ." This means every thought—both good and bad—must align with Christ.

Recently I received a call from clinician who I had not spoken to in a while. We chatted for a bit about our family and life in general. She then told me she was working with an officer from another agency who had a very similar case as me. "You were a success story" she told me. "Can I give him your phone number, and maybe he can call you? I think it will help him."

I responded with a resounding "of course" because I would do anything to help another officer. I've been there and may be able to witness to God's saving grace. Unfortunately, he never called me. Two days later, I learned that an officer from an agency neighboring my old department had jumped off a bridge and was missing. I texted my clinician to tell her I was so sorry to hear about the officer and I asked if that was the one she wanted to give my number to. As I watched my phone text messages, I saw the (...) of her typing. What followed surprised me but, at the same time, it didn't.

"Yes...It was," she said.

This truly broke my heart. I wish he had called me, or I could have called and spoken to him. I had no idea where he was in his battle or even his spiritual life. Sometimes all it takes is the right word at the right moment to save someone, both their body and their soul.

* * * * *

PTSD is real, so we need to take care and support those affected and respond accordingly. I hope Invisible Wounds somehow makes a difference in the way that departments, state governments, and municipalities take care of police officers when this happens instead of further isolating them and subjecting them to the same experience I had. Responder's should not have to fight for benefits and defend their own integrity as they are essentially placed on trial, like a suspect, to fight for benefits. During this process, I had to sit in front of department and town administration while their legal agents insulated that I was lying, weak, greedy, or all of the above. I cannot tell how painful that was to endure. We need to do something now about this dilemma in our country; legislation needs to be passed on both the state and federal levels and fix the process for getting benefits and coverage.

When all else fails, if you read this book, then you are most likely a believer in the Most High, and you will learn to rely on God. I don't care if this book produces one dime of profit as long as it draws awareness to the issue and above all to God. As I leave law enforcement, I am proud of my service. At this point, I am no longer bitter, just disappointed at the way everything transpired, but this is a reminder not to place our faith in man. I pray for all those in my position to receive renewal and restitution.

Spread the word, spread the message.

God bless.

ACKNOWLEDGMENTS

First and foremost I would like to thank my wife, Francesca, for standing beside me when she was probably scared and confused herself with this sudden change in our lives. People often forget how difficult PTSD can be on a spouse, who has to be a part of and witnesses the up-and-down roller coaster moments of sadness, guilt, and agitation. Thank you for enduring my nightmare outbursts and unintentional kicks and swearing while sleeping in bed.

To my daughters, you were so little when writing this, and I am sorry if I was ever short and/or impatient at times. I hope someday you will understand.

To my mother, who endured countless phone calls over the years of policing from me and who I undoubtedly caused additional stress and worry to. This is a testament that a mother's burden and love never ceases. Thank you for being a role model for living righteously through God.

To Becky, my clinician, I was so nervous talking to a clinician for the first time, yet you made me feel so comfortable. You went way above the number of times you were required to meet with me, being there weekly through my entire process, listening to me pour out to you about my life and career. It takes a special person to balance their own life and hardships, then listen to the troubles of other's while still showing you genuinely care. I thank you for the friendship you showed me and your determination to see me through this.

To the rest of my medical support staff, I could not ask for a better psychiatrist and primary care doctor.

To my friends that intermittently checked on me, thank you,

I am sure it was awkward not knowing when or when not to reach out. Just know that any contact is good contact when someone is feeling rejected or alone.

My proofreader, Becky Distefano for volunteering her services.

Lastly to my editor, Christy, who had to read, evaluate, and edit a book that was written by a cop. This should need no explanation. As a first-time author, sharing my very intimate and personal experiences, I appreciate how you made the process very easy, acting not only as an editor but an ally and agent displaying the favor of God.

ABOUT THE AUTHOR

After graduating from Roger Williams University, Nicholas Anthony received a commission as an officer in the US Army and served in the National Guard. That summer after college, at just twenty-two years old, Nicholas began his career in law enforcement in a large New England town. During his time on the force, he was a firearms and tactics instructor, for which he still enjoys a passion today. Upon completing his twelfth year of service, Nicholas was diagnosed with severe PTSD after experiencing frequent physical and mental issues that year.

Being a casual Christian believer, the subsequent pain from the guilt, shame, and fear surrounding certain experiences during his career in law enforcement led him to the Bible for answers. What Nicholas found in Scripture helped him navigate his way through a spiritual battleground, including facing his sins, discovering faith, and conquering fear. Determined to raise awareness and help other police officers struggling with PTSD, Nicholas turned his anger and shame into therapy and put it on paper. Led and heavily assisted by the Holy Spirit, because cops are generally not that eloquent with words, this book became a reality.

Certified in Critical Incident Stress Debriefing and Law Enforcement Chaplaincy, Nicholas continues to help others better understand PTSD. He lives in Florida with his wife and two beautiful, strong-willed daughters.

OFFICERNICHOLASANTHONY.COM

INVISAWOUNDS34@GMAIL.COM

Made in the USA
Monee, IL
27 January 2023

26428031R00133